THE BYZANTINE TRADITION

MAJOR TRADITIONS OF WORLD CIVILIZATION

UNDER THE EDITORSHIP OF HAYDEN V. WHITE

THE BYZANTINE TRADITION

D. A. MILLER

THE UNIVERSITY OF ROCHESTER

Harper & Row, Publishers

NEW YORK AND LONDON

 For information address Harper & Row, Publishers, Incorporated, 49 East 33rd Street, New York, N.Y. 10016.

LIBRARY OF CONGRESS CATALOG CARD NUMBER: 66-14169

CONTENTS

INTRODUCTION

By the end of the fifth century A.D., the Roman state had completely collapsed, and the entire Mediterranean world was thrown into a crisis that was at once political, social, economic, and spiritual. The Romans had given order, stability, and prosperity to the peoples occupying the shores of the Mediterranean Sea, and when Rome went down before the Germanic invaders, it seemed to many people as if the whole world had come to an end. Still, in the midst of this agony and despair, men continued to hope for a rebirth of political leadership and to search for new means of re-establishing social balance. And they continued to look for spiritual guidance, some way to give a meaning to a life that appeared increasingly painful and devoid of purpose and direction.

Out of the maelstrom there ultimately arose two great cultures which offered comprehensive solutions to the fundamental problems of human existence and provided programs of spiritual and material regeneration to a distracted humanity. These were the Muslim culture, a creation of the Arabic peoples inspired by a dynamic new religion, Islam; and the Byzantine culture, a creative synthesis of ideas and institutions that were Greek, Roman, and Oriental. The Muslims, expanding rapidly out of the Arabian Peninsula during the seventh century, came to dominate the southern shores of the Mediterranean, from the Fertile Crescent to Spain.

The Byzantines, from their center in the Anatolian Peninsula (present-day Turkey), radiated out to encompass the Balkans and parts of Russia to the north, Italy to the east, and much of North Africa to the south. It was inevitable that these two great cultures collide, interact, and conflict during their periods of most intense growth. And for nearly a thousand years they vied with one another for complete control of the Mediterranean world. In the end Islam prevailed over Byzantium, but Byzantine cultural forms continued to survive in the Near East after the

Muslim conquest; and in the Slavic world these forms actually continued to evolve and prosper. During the period of contest between Islam and Byzantium, however, these two cultural complexes showed such power and inventiveness that the European civilization which was taking shape simultaneously in the West appeared provincial, not to say barbaric, by comparison with them.

In the late Middle Ages, the Europeans, impelled by forces that were material and spiritual, penetrated those areas that had once been dominated by Byzantine and Muslim. By trade, crusade, and military conquest, the Western Europeans gradually transformed the entire Mediterranean basin into a sphere of European control and influence. But they did not succeed in their efforts to "Westernize" them. The inhabitants of the eastern and southern Mediterranean remained loyal to their own cultural traditions, even when the material advantages of emulating the European way of life seemed most apparent. The impact of Byzantium and Islam had been definitive in setting the mold of the Mediterranean cultural pattern.

The Mediterranean basin is a place where three different cultural traditions still meet, interact, and unfortunately, conflict. In fact, in our own century those parts of the world once dominated by Byzantium and Islam have undergone something approximating true renascences. They have begun to reassert themselves as living traditions, to recover their distinctive voices, and to speak with a confidence that only a profound sense of continuity with a great culture of the past can breed.

In the current cultural dialogues, the world of Islam speaks in a proud and aggressive voice, while that part of the world which descends from Byzantium speaks more softly. This is as it should be, for the life-style of Byzantium in its heyday was nothing if not subtle, while that of Islam has always been assertive in its most creative periods. This difference in life-style may account for the Muslim triumph over Byzantium in the fifteenth century, for when genuine cultural achievement is coupled with militancy, it provides a power that is difficult to counter by finesse alone. This difference may also account for the fact that we have only lately come to appreciate fully the unique contributions which Byzantium made, not only to those parts of the world which it directly controlled, but also to our own cultural tradition in the West.

The influence of Byzantium on the Slavic world is easily discernible; the Byzantines provided the Slavic peoples with institutions, ideas, a religion, and a literary strategy that have borne rich fruits since the fall of Constantinople over five hundred years ago. But in the West, always prone to proclaim its uniqueness as a civilization, we have tended to ignore or to play down this debt. We have no difficulty recognizing that we owe Byzantium for the transmission of the Greek literary and philosophical traditions; had it not been for the preservation of Greek learning and literature in the Eastern Empire, our own fifteen-century Renaissance probably would have taken a profoundly different turn. But it is often forgotten that *how* we approach Greek culture is also in very large part a result of what Western scholars learned from their Byzantine teachers. Similarly, we remember that the great Byzantine theologians made important contributions to the Western understanding of Christian thought and experience; but we tend to forget that Roman Catholic religious ritual and Protestant theology are in very significant ways either conscious or unconscious continuations of certain Byzantine traditions. These are only two of the ways that Byzantium has influenced Western civilization directly. It has influenced it indirectly in many more ways, as a literary inspiration, as a dream, as a model, etc.

If necessary, one could make a case for the study of Byzantine civilization on more pragmatic grounds. We often speak of Byzantium as the perfect example of "caesaropapism" and it is sometimes presented as the prototype of the modern totalitarian state, especially of the Russian state as it has developed since the Revolution of 1917. But it makes more sense to study Byzantium as the prototype of the modern multinational, or transnational state—the state which is made up of many different national and linguistic groups and which is held together by a combination of technological and ideological devices, rather than by a single cultural tradition or by natural boundaries and pressures. Such states have emerged, not only in Russia, but also in the United States, India, and Southeast Asia in our own time. It is possible, therefore, that we can come to understand our own contemporary political experience better if we understand how Byzantium came into being, thrived, and declined during its thousand-year rule over the eastern Mediterranean world in the Middle Ages.

In his contribution to this series, Dr. D. A. Miller of the Department of History at the University of Rochester, has attempted a brief characterization of both the spirit and the practice of Byzantine cultural life from the time of the fall of Rome to the fall of Constantinople in 1453. It is as sparkling as a Byzantine mosaic, and just as carefully crafted. He has not only surveyed the salient events of Byzantine history during this thousand-year period, but he has tried also to render something of the spiritual attitudes that underlay it and inspired its main forms of expression. And he has provided a key to an understanding of a tactic by which the Byzantines succeeded in befuddling their friends and enemies for generations: the tactic of revealing enough of a thing to intrigue the barbarian while leaving enough obscured to awe and confuse him.

Professor Miller's essay has four principal parts. After a brief introduction to the main problems of Byzantine history, he deals, in section 2, with Byzantium considered as the major *Christian* successor to the defunct Roman Empire during the early Middle Ages. Here he discusses the problems that confronted the Byzantines in their foreign enemies—barbarian, Muslim, and European. His discussion of these problems allows him to erect the skeleton of critical political events in terms of the four great dynasties of rulers which presided over Byzantium's rise and fall. And he indicates the crucial role played by the imperial office in the Byzantine solutions to their problems. He shows how various emperors interpreted their dual roles as both administrative heads of state and as image, or representative, of the divine power on earth. Whereas in Western Europe and Islam political and religious power were often divided, in theory or in fact, Byzantium managed to keep them united in a single office—that of the emperor. This gave extraordinary flexibility and prestige to the imperial office, but it also subjected the occupant of it to extraordinary pressures and made fantastic psychological demands upon him. Thus, Professor Miller suggests that an understanding of the Byzantine state is necessary for any study of Byzantine culture, for the strengths as well as the weaknesses of Byzantium were reflected in the office which made it work from the beginning.

Miller then outlines the main achievements of the most important Byzantine rulers. He characterizes the ways in which the various rulers interpreted their roles as both administrative heads of state and religious leaders of Christendom. And as he moves from his account of the Heraclidean springtime to the melancholy of the Palaeologan twilight, he shows how a culture undergoes a shift of mood as its original offensive vigor fades and it assumes a defensive posture.

This survey sets the stage for Miller's discussion of the inner workings of the Byzantine administrative system in section 3. First, Miller indicates the main components of the Byzantine "constitution" or body social—the citizens, the church, and the army—and how they were interrelated. He stresses the highly pragmatic nature of Byzantine society, and shows how the Byzantines managed to balance highly unstable forces which, on occasion, succeeded in overthrowing dynasties, individual emperors, and magistrates—all in the name of God's will and in the conviction that whatever succeeded was right. He thereby dispells the clichés still current among those not familiar with Byzantine culture, that it was "rigid" and "formalistic" in its essence. And he thus prepares the ground for his excellent discussion in detail of the Byzantine imperial office.

Here again Miller distinguishes between theory and practice and characterizes the imperial office as a collection of political and religious functions and symbols. He sees the office as the focal point of highly irrational attitudes among the populace and as one which united the leader with his subjects in often totalitarian ways. He suggests the advantages that such an office could confer on a talented politician, but he makes clear the corrosive effects which that power could have on any man who was neither a genius nor a saint, or who lacked advisors with sufficient talent to make up for the emperor's deficiencies.

He then moves to a consideration of the emperor's immediate environment, his court, and the bureaucracy which the emperor headed and which received its power from him. In his description of the bureaucracy in particular, he shows how the Byzantines had found the middle way between hard-headed realism in the administration of a vast, amorphous empire and the idealism suggested by the ornate, often clumsy, ceremonial rituals which gave to the empire the semblance of perfect form, order, and harmony to the outsider.

It is only then, in section 4, that he tries to analyze the most complex and elusive aspect of Byzantine cultural life: Byzantine Christianity. This was the most powerful spiritual force in the culture and it is the most difficult for the modern Westerner to understand. The Byzantine religion provided the spiritual cement of the empire and of Byzantine cultural life. It joined together peoples with radically dissimilar linguistic and ethnic backgrounds and fused them into a single community. It provided a bridge between Byzantium and Western Europe which allowed for periodic, though often stormy, alliances between them against the common enemy, Islam. And its doctrines and dogmas served as informing presuppositions of most of the creations of Byzantine higher culture, in art, literature, music, and thought.

Of special importance for any preliminary understanding of Byzantine Christianity is the work of the great Alexandrian theologians, Greek religious thinkers who provided the main explanations of the Christian faith in terms congenial to the peoples of the eastern Mediterranean. Miller stresses the spiritualism of Eastern Christianity, its tendency to ignore specific kinds of problems which arose in the administration of church affairs, to leave such affairs to the political power, and to concentrate on the mystical aspects of the faith alone. In the West, the breakdown of the Roman state forced bishops and priests to become involved in the political affairs of their communities, to serve as leaders of their peoples in all kinds of practical activities, and this turned Western religious thought along distinctly worldly lines. This raised with urgency the problem of the proper relationship between church and state, when the state was reborn in the West during Carolingian times; and it resulted in endless debates over the power and prestige of the various orders—lay, priestly, and monastic—in the church hierarchy.

Such issues were discussed in Byzantium, but since the political authority had descended in a virtually unbroken line from the time of the Caesars, the Eastern Church had developed within the protective custody of the state, and it accepted the role played by the emperor in church affairs very early. Relieved from having to take the main role in the direction of the political and social lives of the Eastern Empire, the Byzantine churchmen did not, on the whole, address themselves in a very concentrated or consistent way to the problem of relating Christian dogma to practical daily life. Instead, they investigated with special subtlety the mystical elements in Christianity, excelled in the poetic treatment of the mysteries which underlay and completed the Christian experience of the world, and created a religious tradition that is still regarded as a model of aesthetic otherworldliness.

This high spiritualism of Byzantine Christianity was reflected in the great gap which the Byzantines perceived to exist between the divine and human spheres. It was reflected in church ritual, which, through an assault on the senses of the communicant—by music, chant, incense, light, and color—transported him into another dimension, where he was stripped of the tiresome burden of his reason and his will, and where he could imagine that he had attained a union with the divine every bit as profound as that experienced by the full-time mystic.

The overriding mysticism of Eastern Christianity had a practical function in the life of the empire, although it should not be thought that the mystical element was encouraged for primarily practical reasons. By stressing the essentially mysterious nature of Christianity, the Byzantines discouraged that endless wrangling over fine theological points that might encourage dissent, heresy, and schism in the church, and revolution in the empire. In the cloudy world of the spirit, all worldly differences disappeared, everyone enjoyed the same divine benefits, all were equal.

This leveling tendency was reflected in the liturgy and in the hierarchy: the layman received communion in both kinds and the distinction between layman and priest was played down rather than emphasized, as in the West. The tendency to break down distinctions also showed itself in Byzantine Christology and thought about man. Eastern theologians, as Professor Miller indicates, tended to merge the figure of the Son, Jesus, with the figure of the Father.

This resulted in turn in a stress upon the human qualities of the Virgin Mary long before a similar development occurred in the West, although the cult of the Virgin never achieved the popularity in the East that it has in the West.

The excessive spiritualism of Eastern Christianity inevitably resulted in the elevation of the prestige of the monk, who seemed to be pursuing the union with the divine much more assiduously than either the priest or the layman; and Byzantine monasticism had profound effect upon those parts of Western Christendom that were exposed to its influences. It also made the monk a somewhat more difficult person to control by the usual political and ecclesiastical disciplines.

How Byzantium gave expression to its highest ideals and aspirations is discussed in the last section of the book, section 5, where art, literature, music, and philosophical thought are analyzed. Beginning with a discussion of the Byzantine icon, Professor Miller then moves to a suggestive treatment of Byzantine conceptions of time and space, perception, and theory of color. His analysis suggests arresting parallels between Byzantine and modern, nonrepresentational art and music.

He then returns to a discussion of such practical "arts" as diplomacy and military strategy, where he argues that the same principles that informed higher culture in Byzantium—the blending of the highly spiritualized with the pragmatic—were prime elements in what he calls the "art of survival." He concludes his essay with an account of the Byzantine conception of history, drawing a picture of the way that the Byzantines conceived themselves as a distinct culture, their relations to what had come before them, and their vision of the future. Here he suggests that the ultimate cause of Byzantine political failure was the tendency of the Byzantines to imagine that time was not real, to deny that the world had an objective reality, or to think that it could be ignored by an exercise of the reason or the will. Here is the moral that can, perhaps, be drawn from reflection upon the essay: however beautiful or compelling may be the achievements of a culture which attempts to "flee from reality," reality itself cannot be denied. The loss of the pragmatic element was fatal to Byzantium, but it continues to survive in the spirit of those cultures that draw upon it for models, analogues, or inspiration.

HAYDEN V. WHITE

A PARTIAL CHRONOLOGY

330	Founding of Constantinople by Constantine the Great
395	Death of Theodosius; Eastern and Western parts of the Empire split between his sons.
451	Council of Chalcedon; sharpening of Monophysitic quarrel
527–565	Reign of Justinian; attempted "renovation" of the old Roman Empire
610–711	Heraclid Dynasty: Heraclius to Justinian II
718	Defeat of most serious Arab attempt to take Constantinople by Leo III
717–802	Isaurian Dynasty: Leo III to Irene. The Iconoclastic Controversy
843	Final restoration of icons; end of iconoclasm
860	Russian raiders appear before Constantinople for first time
867–1025	Macedonian Dynasty; Basil I to Basil II
969	Fall of Antioch to Byzantines; height of drive against caliphate
989	Conversion of Vladimir of Kiev to Christianity
1054	Beginning of Schism between Eastern and Western churches
1071	Battle of Manzikert
1095	First Crusade
1176	Battle of Myriocephalon; Byzantine defeat at hands of Seljuk Turks
1204	Fourth Crusade; capture of Constantinople by Crusaders
1261	Recapture of Constantinople
1259–1453	Palaeologan Dynasty: Michael VIII to Constantine XI
1453	29 May 1453; final Turkish assault and fall of Constantinople

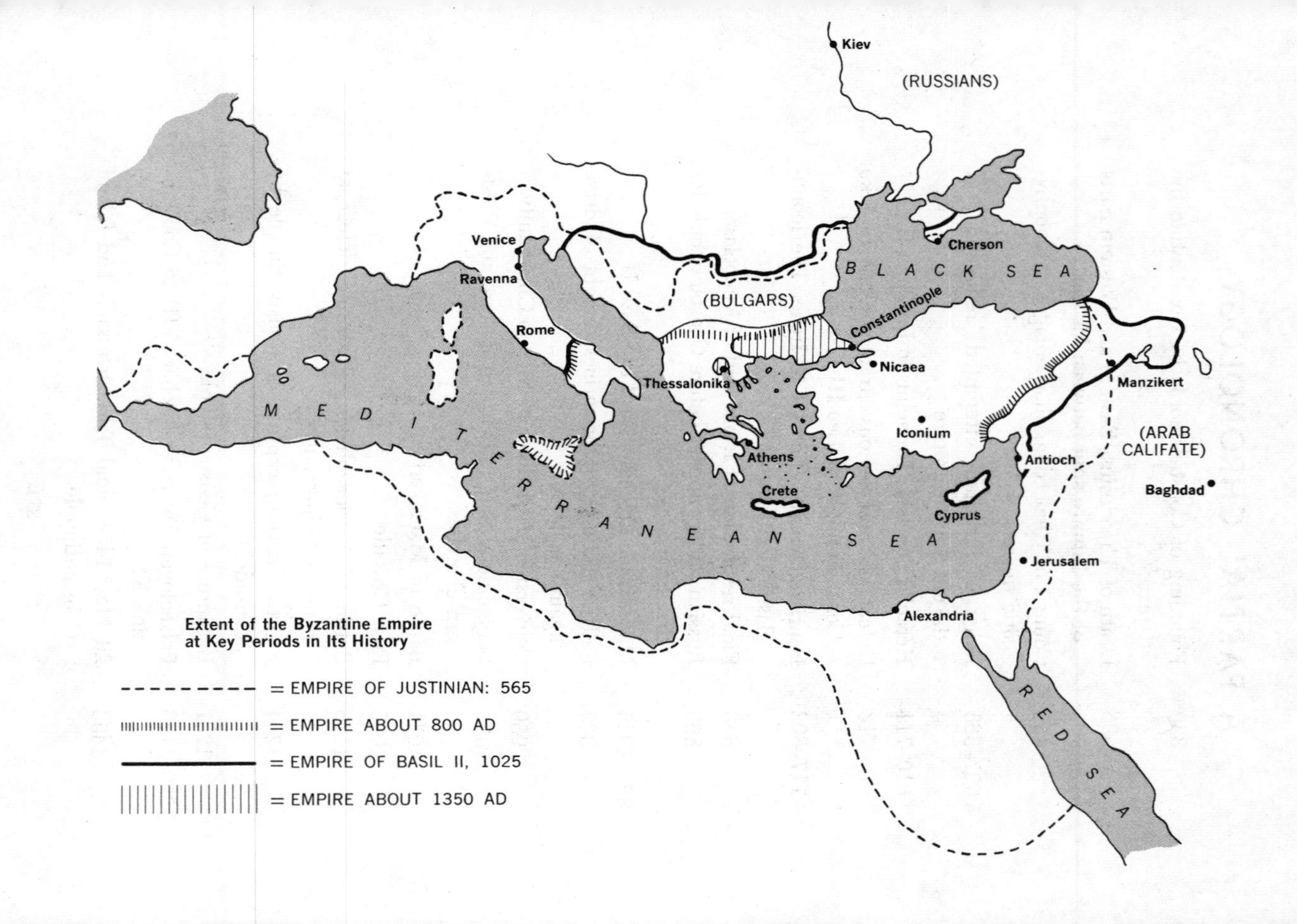

Extent of the Byzantine Empire at Key Periods in Its History

THE BYZANTINE TRADITION

PROBLEMS AND DEFINITIONS

Byzantium and the Historian

Students of the civilizations of the West have only recently turned to the stepchild Byzantium. This seems to have happened because Byzantium, large and long-lived as it was, was masked behind the older classical civilizations of Greece and Rome. Moreover, terms and concepts which describe the older civilizations do not fit the "Later Empire" at all, and even on the most elementary level Byzantium is still a shadowy and myth-ridden name. We think of the orator and athlete of Greece, the legionary and magistrate of Rome—but what types represent this polity, which endured for three times as long as the principate of Augustus, and ten times as long as Athens' democracy?

The clichés which too often come to mind—the weak but bloodstained emperor, the sly and cynical eunuch—are unsympathetic reverberations from the eighteenth and nineteenth centuries; we might collect them as curiosities, but they hinder rather than help us understand Byzantium. As historians, we should prefer to have the Byzantines speak for themselves, and yet they seem extraordinarily reluctant to do this. We therefore isolate and label their civilization, using a term which they would never recognize. (Byzantium, or Byzantion, was the old Greek town on the site of which Constantine built New Rome, the City of Constantine, or Constantinople.) These "Byzantines" always referred to themselves as Romans, except late in the history of the Empire, when a resurgence of Greek feeling led them to take up again the old name Hellene (up to this time synonymous with "pagan"). But Greek, not Latin, had been the official administrative and cultural language of the Empire from the sixth century onward. Thus we are confronted by a distinctive body politic descended from and calling itself a Roman empire, with a predominantly Greek culture (that is, the Hellenistic Greek culture of the fourth century B.C. to the fourth century A.D.), and with a state religion that was Christian.

To this strange amalgam we must add another influence, more uncertain still. No element of Byzantine civilization has been more widely discussed and puzzled over than the so-called Oriental element, which has explained (or been blamed for) Byzantine duplicity, ferocity, mysticism, and much of their art, among other traits or products good and bad. The label "Oriental" has been too loosely applied; we may simply say that Byzantium absorbed and transmuted influences from the older centers of civilization within her orbit, including Persia and Syria-Palestine.

The Eternal Empire

What was Byzantium, then, and what has it left us? It was, first of all, a fully articulated and rationalized, truly imperial political structure which maintained itself for more than a millennium. As such, it served as a model for many ambitious states: echoes of it appear in the court circles of the Carolingians, in the tenth-century Ottonian state, in the papacy, and in the elaborate diplomacy of Venice. Powers which actually inherited parts of the Byzantine Empire were more directly affected, such as the Arabs, the Normans in Sicily, and probably the Ottoman Turks. With or without its imitators, however, Byzantium intrigues us because it survived, because it achieved political stability by unique means, and lived out a long life in the face of great odds.

Second, Byzantium was, for all but the last three centuries of its existence, a major military power in the Mediterranean. Obviously, the first point—the Empire's very being—depended on this. Moreover, the development of a distinct western European, Christian culture is inconceivable if we remove the Balkan and Anatolian bastion which Byzantium defended. Much has been made of the Battle of Tours-Poitiers, won by Charles Martel's Franks over the Spanish Saracens in 732, and of what this victory portended for Europe. Against Constantinople, Islam twice threw (after 674 and in 717–718), not a raiding party, but great fleets and armies—the might of Arab Islam at its highest tide. Other attacks, over the centuries, were almost as serious. Byzantium fended them off, as it dispersed and controlled the steppe peoples beyond the Danube and held the Arabs in south Italy. Obviously we can never know what would have happened if there had been no Byzantine defense. We only know that we are the heirs of a world which, for centuries, was allowed to grow and find strength behind a shield provided, in great part, by the Byzantine Empire.

Finally, there is the cultural phenomenon of Byzantium. The conservatism, the closed vision which is so much in contrast to Europe before and after the Renaissance, has cut Byzantium off from us—and yet if Byzantium had *not* conserved, little of the vital classical heritage would have been left to revive in the fourteenth century and later. The Carolingian Renaissance, praised for its recovery of ancient authors, lasted a century; the Byzantines, on their part, held classical literature in honor throughout the life of the Empire, and directly or indirectly saved almost all of the ancients who were to be saved.

But this is a rather narrow view of Byzantine civilization (though one the Byzantines themselves would have cheerfully accepted). In its own right, it was a powerful creation. Its art and architecture charged power with subtlety, and achieved effects that still reach us after many centuries. Its literature, derivative on the surface, is rich; and Byzantium, for all its formalism, was abundant in *personalities*—individuals, revealed in letters, or with their flavor caught in works that show the first hint of autobiography. It is difficult to think of a time when East Rome was what the poet Yeats claimed it to be—a country for old men. The tone of the Empire, which could never be exported or imitated, was not merely magnificent: it was vital. The Byzantines were, after all, Greeks; they were eternally possessed of the urge to find order and the Golden Mean, and then to disrupt it.

THE CHRISTIAN EMPIRE

The World Power (330—1025)

The Roman Emperors to Justinian

The founding of Constantinople, the City of Constantine, by the emperor whose name it took, established two facts clearly. First, the eastern provinces of the Roman Empire required their own permanent administrative center. Second, Christianity was not to be merely one among the many accepted religions of a tolerant state, for Constantinople was founded specifically as a Christian capital city.

In setting up a second Rome, in 330 A.D., Constantine was not moving without precedent. The ponderous machinery of Roman government had been reformed by his predecessor Diocletian, especially with an eye to more efficient and closer control of the East, with its special problems, political and cultural. He did not "divide the Empire," for that was unthinkable. Yet now a second capital city existed in fact, even if only one man held the imperial office, and that city was obviously different from the old capital. It might have its own seven hills, a Senate House, forums, pagan statues, and all the other material echoes of the first Rome; but it was dedicated, as well, to the Christians' God, and it would be the focus of a *Christian* Empire.

All this would emerge clearly only in the future. For the successors of Constantine and the others who came to the East Roman throne for the next two centuries there was only one Empire, and they were its custodians. The last of them, Justinian (527–565), even undertook to reunite the parts sundered by the Germanic invasions. With his failure the history of a "Byzantine" empire can properly be said to begin.

The first task of those who ruled from Constantinople was to avoid or defend themselves against the external threats and internal weaknesses which eventually brought the western provinces, and old Rome, down. Obviously, they would have been happy to save the entire Empire, but they could not. The East appeared sounder than the West for a number of reasons. Without involving ourselves in the enigma of the "decline and fall" we can note the following:

1. The greatest thrust of the barbarian Germanic tribes in the fourth and fifth centuries was against the West. The Eastern emperors, in fact, were not above pushing these barbarians (such as the Visigoths and Ostrogoths) westward by a combination of force and diplomacy. The East was not, therefore, seriously disrupted by invasion or permanently occupied.

2. The Eastern provinces, especially the Asian, formed a stronger economic base than anything in the West. Egypt was still a productive granary; the Syrian coastlands were active mercantile centers; Asia Minor was a priceless reservoir of manpower. The East, therefore, remained much more resilient than the West under the fearsome load of

taxation which provided the means to defend the frontiers and administer the machinery of government.

3. The military crisis which finally rendered the West incapable of defending itself was avoided in the East—partly by pure luck. This crisis made itself felt throughout the Empire principally because of the scarcity of native-born recruits, who were replaced by expensive, and untrustworthy, barbarian mercenaries. The Eastern emperors used mercenaries and mercenary generals, but unlike their colleagues in the West, they managed to keep from becoming completely dependent on them, and by the sixth century had moved to limit their use.

These and other arguments can be used to explain the survival of the eastern provinces. The undeniable fact is that they did survive; that from the death of Theodosius the Great, in 395, a separate imperial line ruled in Constantinople; that whatever the theory of the unity of the Roman world, the potency of that world was concentrated here. The men on the imperial throne had to minister especially to the particular problems of the East.

The greatest of these problems was religious, not political, and the emperor had to be deeply involved in these religious problems. Why that was so we will see later. For the moment, we shall merely note that it was accepted that he had to assist his subjects in defining the truths of Christianity. (By the fifth century it was assumed that his subjects *were* almost all Christians.) When theologians disagreed, the emperor had to make clear the path to salvation.

Unfortunately, the imperial decisions were not always taken as final, and the result was a series of violent controversies which were never finally settled. One of the most serious of these controversies was between Orthodoxy and Monophysitism, which centered on the exact relationship of the divine and human elements in the incarnate Christ. Final definitions were attempted through church councils, such as that at Chalcedon in 451, and by imperial edicts. Nothing worked, especially not the edicts which tried to find a compromise position and then forbade any further debate on the subject. Only the Arab conquests of the seventh century brought an end, by stripping away those provinces—Egypt and Syria—most zealously opposed to compromise.

The religious consciousness which led to the Monophysitic controversy was one of the special conditions which affected the government of the East. Another was the heritage of Greek language and cultural leadership, as opposed to the Latin traditions of the West. The "Roman" emperors who sat in Constantinople had to be influenced by the fact that they ruled in the East, even as they tacitly accepted the removal of the Western provinces from the Empire. However, the gradual disappearance of the old, unitary imperial view was abruptly reversed when, in 527, Justinian took the throne.

The nephew of an illiterate soldier-emperor from Illyria, Justinian himself was a cultivated and devoted servant of Roman tradition. His goal was no less than to restore the Roman Empire physically and spiritually. His greatest success was the definitive compilation of Roman law which still bears his name, the Code of Justinian; his greatest failure, the thirty years of war which he waged to take back North Africa, Spain, and especially Italy from the Germanic dynasties which were in power there. Justinian, a complex and ambitious man married to a fascinating woman, the Empress Theodora, invariably catches at our imagination. But the plain truth was that the resources of the East were not enough to support the reconquest of all the old Roman world. Justinian's vision faded, and his wars left the Eastern

Empire weakened against the massive attacks of old and new enemies. After Justinian, came the long defense, and with it the growth of separate institutions and a distinctly new civilization still clinging to the old Roman name. Justinian himself, the last "Roman" emperor, erected the monument which became one of the symbolic focuses of that new civilization, the great "Byzantine" cathedral of Hagia Sophia.

PERSIANS AND ARABS; SLAVS, AVARS, AND BULGARS

The physical safety of the Eastern Empire was at all times threatened from two directions: first from the southeast, marked by the Syrian marches and the mountains rimming the Anatolian Plateau; and second from the north, along the Danube and on a line drawn westward through the Balkan mountains. The prime concern of Byzantine foreign policy was to keep peace on at least one of these fronts at all times. Against a concerted attack on both, the Empire could not long stand.

In the south the Byzantines faced their most powerful civilized antagonists, Persians and Arabs. With the Persian Empire under its Sassanid dynasty the Byzantines had a peculiar and ambivalent relationship. How could there be *two* world empires? Yet the Persians held to a tradition of rule which they felt was older than the Roman power by centuries, harking back to the great house of Darius the Great and Xerxes. Their divinely appointed rulers, supported by an elaborate bureaucracy and court structure, were also served by a jealous, monotheistic state-supported cult, Zoroastrianism. Persia was rich, populous, and dangerous; in the third and fourth centuries Rome had found it necessary to post almost half its military strength in the East in order to secure the frontier there. Throughout the fifth century the two powers were at peace, but in the sixth century war came again, and built to a crescendo in the latter part of the century. It became clear that the Persian King of Kings, Chosroes II, was intent on eliminating the anomalous East Roman Empire entirely. Faced with incessant barbarian attacks in the north and a war of annihilation in the south, Byzantium put its faith in the Emperor Heraclius (610–641) newly come to the throne in the teeth of the crisis. Heraclius accepted severe defeats, the loss of Syria and even Jerusalem, then returned with a reformed army to hurl the Persians back. By 638 the successors of Chosroes were calling themselves sons and slaves of the Roman emperor.

All this was to be in vain, however. While Persia and East Rome ravaged each others' lands and decimated each others' armies, a new religious and national power was growing in a forgotten corner of the world. The faith which the self-styled "last Prophet of God," Mohammed, preached in north Arabia in the early seventh century, appeared, like Christianity in its earliest phase, to be a sort of offshoot of Judaism. It was severely monotheistic, legalistic, puritanical, and it set flame to Arab tribes trained by centuries of raid and border warfare. Barely united under Islam ("the way of submission"), the Arab tribes raided north, and found immediately that no effective resistance met them. Not only were both Persia and East Rome completely exhausted, but the Syrian and Egyptian provinces proved disinclined to defend themselves. The people were disaffected on religious grounds, being Monophysites and therefore heretics, and on cultural grounds as well. The Arab, to them, was preferable to the Greek heirs of Rome. Syria fell to Islam, followed by almost all the territories of the Persian Empire, then Egypt. The North African provinces held out only for a while longer. By the middle of the seventh century the East, except for Asia Minor, was in Arab hands.

From this point to the early tenth century, Byzantium and the Arab power faced each other across the Taurus mountains. Before the frontier was stabilized the Empire had to endure blows which were almost fatal, including two full-scale attacks by land and sea against Constantinople itself. After this, the two states settled down to permanent watchfulness interspersed by raiding in season. A great part of the effectiveness of the Byzantine defense of their southern frontier was owed to military and administrative reforms usually attributed to Heraclius, but begun before him and fully developed after his reign. This reform, the institution of the system of "themes" (a new name for provinces) had two main characteristics: the concentration of both civil and military power in the hands of a military officer, and the settling of soldiers, especially heavy cavalrymen, on land granted by the state in return for military service. Both as an economic and as a military reform the results were good, especially in Asia Minor.

Though there could be no peace with the caliphate, the religious state set up by the Arabs, the long years of contact brought about an inevitable diffusion of influences from one power to the other, especially since the Arabs showed a remarkable ability to borrow from older civilizations and to create their own synthesis, a synthesis from which Byzantium, in turn, borrowed more than is usually realized. On the northern frontier, however, Byzantium faced a succession of enemies who had very little to give except the edge of the sword, and who proved to be at once dangerous foes and apt pupils of the Empire. These were the masses of Slavs, and with them, usually at their head, Turkic-speaking peoples in successive waves.

The ultimate causes of the migrations which broke over the Danubian frontier in the late sixth century must be looked for in central Asia. The great march of the Hunnic hordes, culminating in the career of Attila (d. 453), was followed by other movements; spasms moving westward across the south Russian steppe. In the late sixth century the invading Turks, fighting in the Hunnic fashion with light horse-archers, were called Avars. With them were swarms of Slavic-speaking barbarians. The Avars eventually retreated beyond the Danube, but the Slavs stayed, and the Balkan Peninsula was lost to the Empire.

These Slavs had appeared in Attila's time. There were numbers of them in south Russia, and they moved behind and among better-organized peoples. Their strength lay in their numbers and their very lack of organization; they moved like a tide, not dramatically but inevitably. And they were very quick at their lessons.

After the Avars came other Turks. The Bulgars (several varieties were distinguished) made permanent settlements south of the Danube in the second half of the seventh century and proved to be powerful and persistent antagonists. Their Turkish military aristocracy was gradually absorbed into the Slavic matrix, but the Bulgar threat remained and grew worse. The Khazars settled on the Volga and were, for three centuries, the key to Byzantine policies regarding the steppes, for they could strike in many directions; it was worthwhile to keep their good will. The late-arriving Magyars, who moved into the Carpathian plain in the ninth century, were the only one of these peoples to retain their language and identity in the midst of the Slavs. With all of these, and with such others as the Slavic nations on the western edge of the Balkan peninsula, the Empire had to deal one way or another: by force, guile, or persuasion.

HERACLIDS, ISAURIANS, AMORIANS, MACEDONIANS

The task of defending and administering the Empire during 500 years of survival, growth, and eventual triumph fell to the men, and women, of four remarkable dynasties: the Heraclids, the Isaurian house, the Amorians, and the Macedonians—all springing, significantly, from the Anatolian heartland, and three of the four (the Heraclids, Amorians, Macedonians) of Armenian stock. Of them the Amorians ruled for only 50 years; the Macedonians for almost 200. The latter had the good fortune to rule at the peak of the Empire's course, and we know more about them; we know least about the history of the Heraclid house. We know that these four families, with their adopted and co-opted assistants, included a considerable number of talented individuals. This was well for the Empire, for no matter how well- or ill-served these emperors were, the responsibilities of rule fell ultimately on them alone, and their abilities had to be thrown into the balance. We can conclude that most of them passed their tests, and they were tested often.

The Heraclids—the five generations who succeeded the Emperor Heraclius—had the unenviable job of picking up and saving what remained after the Arabs had struck off some of the most prosperous and valuable parts of the Empire. Unfortunately, our written sources on the seventh century are unusually sparse. This is a pity, for we suspect that serious and far-reaching changes in administration, economic and social relationships, and even in the very concept of the imperial office were effected in this century. We do know that the Empire endured grave moments, so grave that at one point the Emperor Constans II (641–668) was ready to move the center of administration to the West, to Sicily, and leave the East to the Arabs and the barbarian scavengers. But the Arabs were eventually fended off, and even set back sharply, and the Slavs temporarily pacified.

The last representative of this effective but erratic dynasty was the man who might stand as a caricature of the "typical" Byzantine emperor: Justinian II (685–695, 705–711). Devout, a good administrator and soldier, he dedicated the first of his two separate reigns to proving his abilities; his second (after a conspiracy had removed him and he had been mutilated) to showing a gift for almost manic cruelty. Few regretted his end, but his house had done its work of reconstruction and consolidation well. By the beginning of the eighth century the tone of the Empire was firmer and its morale was high.

In 717 the first of the Isaurian emperors, Leo III, took the throne, and as soon as his position was reasonably secure he led the Empire into a controversy which has exercised modern historians almost as much as it excited the Byzantines of the eighth century: the quarrel over images (the "iconoclastic" question). The controversy centered on the use in churches of representations—icons—of the sacred figures of Christianity: Christ himself, Mary, the Apostles and saints. The Isaurian emperors objected to the fact that these icons were being worshiped in a fashion which smacked of idolatry, and they ordered the offensive pictures (the Byzantines very rarely produced sculpture in the round) removed. They were fanatically supported by most of the army, which was mainly from Asia Minor, and by many of the secular clergy. They were fanatically opposed by the monks and by many of the commoners.

Why did the Isaurians strike at images? Leo III, the founder, hailed from southern Asia Minor. Was he affected by Moslem influences? Certainly the iconoclastic doctrines had a strong puritanical element. Was the move made to tighten imperial control of the church? Or was the whole series of measures aimed at the growing power of the monastic clergy? All these suggestions may have some truth in them. The Isaurians did devote much time and energy to cutting back the power, and the numbers, of monks, on the grounds that they were nonproductive. (Since the historians of the period were monkish chroniclers, it can be imagined what sort of picture we have been left of the Isaurian emperors.)

The iconoclastic rulers moved against image-worship with every means at their disposal. Monasteries were dissolved and their monks returned to the world by force, patriarchs were appointed or dismissed, pressure was brought to bear on the Bishop of Rome, and eventually a general Church Council was called (754) to draw up the definitive doctrines of iconoclasm. In all of this the son of Leo, Constantine V (741–775), was even more zealous than his father. However, not all of Constantine's considerable vitality was devoted to pursuing icon-worshipers. Leo had broken the last great Arab assault of 717–718; now his son campaigned vigorously against the caliphate. Against the Bulgars, Constantine was even more successful; the blows he dealt them halted their attacks for a generation. More than a century later the common people of the capital remembered Constantine as a champion against the Bulgars, and in a moment of new peril called on him to return to them from his tomb.

After Constantine's death the impetus of iconoclasm lessened. Leo IV ruled briefly and mildly, then died and left the realm to his widow, Irene, who acted as regent. Irene (780–802) was only one of a number of remarkable Byzantine women. A zealous image-worshiper, possessed of toplofty ambition and few moral scruples, she worked to advance her own power and, incidentally, the cause of images. She plotted and survived plots, blinded and deposed her own son, and was finally removed by a palace coup headed by bureaucrats who saw that both her foreign and domestic policies were turning out disastrously for the Empire. With her the Isaurian line ended.

The Amorians came to power in 820 after a period of great stress for the Empire, which lost two emperors in battle and barely staggered through a full-scale rebellion. Michael, founder of the house, was an Anatolian and an iconoclast, and he reinstituted a watered-down iconoclasm, but the old vigor had gone out of this doctrinal fight. In 843 orthodoxy, in the form of an acceptable veneration (not worship) of images, had returned. This was by the way, however, for the true significance of the three Amorian emperors lay in the fact that they presided over the beginning of a new expansion of Byzantine energies. The Empire found itself renewed, at a time when the Arab caliphate was losing its effective unity, and the rival Frankish Empire, created by Charlemagne, was proving that it could not sustain his dreams of power in the West. In addition, Byzantium's cultural prestige, always high, was now breaking through into the north, capturing the Slavic Balkans and drawing them into the imperial orbit more and more.

All of these tendencies were well under way in the Amorian period, and continued under the great Macedonian house. Two signal events show the pattern: the advance of Byzantine arms against the Arabs in northern Syria and Mesopotamia and eastern Asia Minor, and the conversion of the Bulgar kingdom to Christianity by Byzantine missionaries. Both occurred during the reign of the last Amorian, Michael III. Almost simultaneously the Empire became aware of a new people, when raiders called *Rōs* attacked Constantinople in 860. More contacts would follow, until eventually Byzantine Christianity would celebrate its greatest missionary triumph, the conversion of "Russia," the principality of Kiev. Great energies—energies of a truly imperial scope—were being brought into play by the Byzantines.

Basil I, called the Macedonian, came to the throne in 867 amid the echo of victories the Amorians and their servants had won. He was actually of Armenian extraction, and this nation would be increasingly prominent in imperial affairs during the Macedonian period. Basil was of low birth, and he eliminated the former emperor in a particularly atrocious manner, but he had a very high opinion of the imperial office itself. The Macedonians, in fact, would develop the theory behind the emperor's power to its fullest extent: in law, in ceremonial and protocol, in foreign relations and diplomacy.

Basil was followed by his son Leo (886–912), called "the Wise" for his learning and his law code, a reworking of the great Justinianic code. Unfortunately, other affairs intruded on the bookish Leo, for in his time the Bulgars, now Christian, proved to be as dangerous as they had ever been as pagans. The Bulgarian tsar, Simeon, contemplated becoming the first ruler of a combined Bulgar-Byzantine empire. Leo could not defeat him and was forced to placate and endure him, but the Empire had outlasted other ambitious foreign princes, and it outlasted Simeon.

Leo left the throne to his brother and young son, and the boy, Constantine VII, was soon left to rule alone under a regency. This always ticklish situation was eventually turned to account by the *Drungarius* (High Admiral) of the Fleet, Romanus Lecapenus. The Lecapeni, like the Macedonians, were Armenian, even poorer born, but Romanus made an excellent co-emperor. Constantine was left to his favorite literary pursuits; Romanus ran the Empire, and his generals led the continuing and increasingly successful counterattack against the Arabs.

By the time Constantine, late in life, came to be emperor in his own right, he had produced some of our most valuable sources dealing with the working of the Byzantine court and state. However, his son Romanus, when he succeeded to the throne, had little time to follow his father's elaborately devised advice, contained, for example, in his treatise "On the Administration of the Empire." In 963 a regency ruled for Romanus' sons. But the momentum of the Byzantine advance had to be directed and controlled; so two experienced soldiers were successively associated with the dynasty by the choice of Romanus' widow. Under Nicephorus Phocas and John Tzimiskes (963–976, including both reigns), the Byzantines achieved their most signal victories over the disintegrating Arab power. Syrian cities lost since the seventh century came back into the Empire; Antioch the Great was taken; even Jerusalem was not beyond reach, though the Byzantines did not advance against it for tactical reasons. Tzimiskes also settled the northern frontier, where an ancient Byzantine diplomatic device—drawing one barbarian on to attack another—had backfired; the Russians, persuaded to threaten the restless Bulgars, had decided to stay on the Danube. Tzimiskes, in a brilliant campaign, winkled them out again. When he died, the military situation of East Rome had never been better.

Basil II (976–1025), the last of the Macedonian emperors, capped the achievements in arms of all his predecessors; hindsight tells us at what cost. In the first part of his reign he had to withstand full-scale civil war led by two powerful generals, representatives of a hostile landed aristocracy; then a new Bulgarian threat arose, and Basil went permanently on campaign. He seems to have enjoyed this as much as he enjoyed anything. He was a grim man, with no taste for the arts, and he never married. By the time he had finished with the Bulgars he had fully justified the name *Bulgaroctonos* (Bulgar-slayer) which the Byzantines gave him, and the Bulgar kingdom was gone.

Basil II died in 1025. The borders of the Byzantine Empire rested again on the Danube. The pagan Russians had been converted to Christianity, and Byzantine influence extended deep into Russia. Arabic Islam seemed to have been shattered forever. If there was a new "Holy Roman Empire" in the West its power and its culture were incomparably less significant than East Rome's. By the late tenth century the Byzantine Empire seemed to have passed beyond all its trials; it blazed in the East, and the Macedonian house gave its name to the brilliance.

The Remnant (1025–1453)

When historians divide the life of a social organism —for example, an empire—into neat divisions of ascendency and decline, growth and decay, they, hopefully, fool no one. The divisions are conventions; the dates, dramatic aids.

In the case of the Byzantine Empire, no one can responsibly claim that at the death of Basil II a sort of plug was pulled, so that the potency of the Byzantine state and civilization drained off with an historically audible gurgle. Yet we know that by the end of the eleventh century severe crises had broken over the Empire, and that the Byzantines were unable to respond successfully. We also know that the death of Basil left the state without effective direction (rule passed to the daughters of Basil's brother after the brother had had a brief reign). We shall never know if the presence of another Basil as energetic as his father would have materially affected the issue. We can only take the year 1025 as a date of some significance, and with that accepted, we can dig into some of the developments which had accompanied and even aided the Byzantine triumph, but which had other and more perilous resonances.

1. From at least the ninth century onward, we can see a stiffening and stratification appearing in the hitherto loosely knit Byzantine society. In opposition to the accepted imperial theory of a truly classless society under the emperor, a self-conscious aristocracy had made its appearance: an aristocracy of blood and birth rather than of honor and office granted by the Throne. During the Macedonian period more and more "great names" appear: landed magnates, usually based in Asia Minor, with vast estates growing vaster in the course of time. The result was a threefold crisis: an economic crisis, a crisis in the morale of the society, and a closely related military problem.

a. The Byzantines had rejuvenated their state by encouraging the growth of the smallholder, especially the peasant soldier, who formed the backbone of the thematic regiments. The collection of a major part of the tax revenues depended on the existence of this class. As the large estates expanded, the smallholders passed from the tax rolls into a dependent, almost feudal, relationship to the magnate. The result was, at the very least, a drop in the revenues of the state.

b. The landed aristocracy began to regard itself as a superior element within, and even separate from, the state. Secure in what had come to be hereditary positions in the military hierarchy of the themes, they developed an antagonism to the court and especially to the imperial bureaucracy. The idea of a career open to talent did not appeal to them. The two great and necessary constituent elements in Byzantine government—army and bureaucracy under the emperor—drew away from one another. One result was open rebellion on the part of the magnates, such as the revolts which took place under Basil II.

c. The particularly dangerous effect of these crises was to weaken the military potential of the Empire, especially when, as after Basil, overoptimism kept the rulers from examining their real position. No weakness had been visible during the tenth century, for the wars of reconquest in Syria and Mesopotamia were much to the taste of the great families, land hungry as they were. Yet Basil II had been forced to recruit mercenaries—6000 Russians loaned by the Grand Prince of Kiev—to win his civil war. And when war came again in the latter part of the eleventh century, the Byzantine army, for all its victorious past, was divided in its loyalties between emperor and generals, was untrustworthy, and was defeated. Moreover, the defeat accentuated its weaknesses. The proud record of the thematic armies ended; the emperor had to have mercenaries—expensive and willful—to fight his battles.

2. To deterioration of the internal fabric of the Empire was added an important and dangerous shift in By-

zantine foreign policy. New power centers were appearing, in the West, and to the south and east, where Turkic converts were rejuvenating Islam, and Byzantium seemed to have neither the strength nor the resilience to accommodate these new forces into its old world-view.

BYZANTIUM AND THE WEST

The Byzantines had kept a sizable foothold in Italy and Sicily from the time when Justinian's generals had conquered the peninsula. The area under Byzantine control was organized into themes like the rest of the Empire. Even if that Empire's chief concerns lay elsewhere, it remained involved in the West.

One point of necessary contact and permanent involvement was in the religious sphere: the Byzantines always kept up relations with the pope, for a Christian Empire could not ignore the foremost representative of the Western Church. The two Romes, however, held increasingly opposite views on essential doctrines, especially on that of the relative religious authority of pope and emperor. Open clashes were not uncommon: a pope was seized and exiled in the seventh century; iconoclasm had been violently opposed by the Holy See, and even after that movement ended there was a crisis over the perennial problem of papal supremacy in the ninth century. An explosion of tempers in the early eleventh century merely showed how far the two points of view had drifted apart. Christianity was not supposed to be divided in two sections after 1054, but it was in fact—more in liturgical forms than in basic assumptions, but still divided.

The Empire was also drawn by necessity into political involvements in Italy and beyond the Alps. Byzantium had to have allies against the Arabs who had begun in the ninth century to push into Sicily, and now held the island and threatened Italy. Therefore, it had extended recognition to the "empire" of Charlemagne and his successors and to the German "empire" of the tenth century, both of which had their interests in Italy. But to the Byzantines, the Franks and the Germans were, and remained, barbarians.

In the early eleventh century a new antagonist appeared in Italy: Norman adventurers eager for land and loot, who rapidly expelled the Arabs, swallowed up most of the Byzantine enclave which remained, and made serious attempts to cross the Adriatic and seize the Balkan Peninsula. This is a partial background to the series of events which forced the Byzantines and the nations of the West to deal with one another, and which culminated in the permanent crippling of East Rome—the Crusades.

All the factors which antedated the launching of these singular expeditions cannot be examined here. For the purpose of this historical sketch we can note that Alexius Comnenus, an able and adroit emperor, was engaged in piecing his empire together, and above all trying to expel the Turks who had established themselves in it. He appealed to the rest of Christendom for mercenaries, and got instead hordes of undisciplined and unwashed Westerners led in part by the Normans whom he had an excellent reason to distrust.

What the Eastern Empire eventually gained from the Crusades, and that only temporarily, was a respite from the Turks and a little territory. Except for this, the coming of the Crusaders brought nothing good. Contact between the two societies resulted in suspicion and open hostility. Greek and Frank disliked each others' political organization, mode of Christianity, military techniques, language, morals, and habits. As long as the Comneni occupied the imperial throne some minimal cooperation was possible, but by the end of the twelfth century an open break seemed imminent.

The result of such divisions and such hatreds was the diversion against Constantinople of an expedition originally intended for the Holy Land. The capital fell in 1204, and Geoffrey de Villehardouin, a Frankish knight who wrote an account of the event, said that never since the Creation had so much loot been seized. The court and its dignitaries fled, the territories of the Empire were divided among Western freebooters in the feudal fashion, and the rites of Latin Christianity were celebrated in the great cathedral. The Byzantines retook the city sixty years later, but never forgot their hatred of the Westerners who had dispossessed them and stripped their chief city. The Crusades, so far as the Eastern Empire was concerned, were an unqualified disaster.

THE DEFENSE AGAINST THE TURKS

The second challenge to the old patterns of Byzantine power came from old enemies in a new disguise. In the tenth century the Arab caliphate had fallen under the influence of Turkish mercenaries originally recruited as a palace guard. By the eleventh century power had shifted completely into the hands of Turkish migrants from central Asia, the Seljuks. The Turkish phase in the history of Islam was now, in fact, begun, and Byzantium soon felt its effects. In 1071 the Emperor Romanus Diogenes took a Byzantine army into the Armenian highlands to meet a raiding force of Seljuk Turks; most of his army fled before contact was made, and the remainder were badly beaten, while the emperor himself was captured, at Manzikert, in eastern Anatolia.

This defeat was no deathblow to the Empire, but the Byzantines seemed unable to rally. Without meeting serious opposition, the Turks breached the frontier barrier which had stood so long. Within a decade they had occupied the entire central Anatolian Plateau and stood within an easy march of Constantinople itself. The capital of the Seljuk Sultanate of Rūm (Rome) was set up at Iconium, in the heart of what had been the most valuable possession of the Empire, its main bulwark and recruiting ground.

The Turks had been aided by the party strife, confusion, and aimless unpreparedness in the capital, but when the strong house of Comnenus took over the government of the Empire, some order was restored. Alexius was able to throw the Normans out of the Balkans and he defeated the Pechenegs, another Turkic steppe people who had crossed the Danube, but against the Seljuks he was unsuccessful. Some lands were recovered during the first stages of the First Crusade, and Alexius' successor John recovered more. Then, a century after Manzikert, John's son Manuel, who had involved the Empire in a number of unfortunate adventures in the West, led a Byzantine army to total destruction at the hands of the Seljuks at Myriokephalon. From *this* disaster there was to be no rebound.

The Seljuk Turks, however, were never to complete their conquest of the Empire they had crippled. The last blows were struck instead by another Turkic people—not a tribe, but a horde of adventurers established in an enclave between Byzantines and Seljuks, calling themselves Osmanli. The Osmanli, or Ottomans, remained permanently at war; they attracted restless warriors from all the Turkish centers, and expanded their holdings steadily. By the mid-fourteenth century they had crossed to Europe, and by the end of that century they had conquered all the Balkans, obliterating the Serbian and Bulgarian principalities in the process. Their advance was briefly halted by an incursion of Mongols into Asia Minor, under Tamerlane, but never by the Byzantines for long. The fact that they could take the capital of the remnant of the Byzantine Empire when they chose, was never really in doubt.

THE PALAEOLOGAN TWILIGHT

The last two centuries of the Empire's existence, like the two centuries of its greatest glory, were presided over by one dynasty. The family of the Palaeologi, like the Macedonians, gave their name to a great cultural and intellectual revival, but in their case this was the only outlet for the creativity of the Byzantines, for politically they were almost helpless.

However, the Palaeologan emperors did their best, and some had ambitions which far overreached the resources of the state. Byzantine diplomacy was as skillful as ever, though there was little force to back it, and the Palaeologi made much use of the diplomatic or "dynastic" marriage to bolster and extend their influence. But in cold fact, Byzantium was an empire no longer, except in name. The insignificant forces of mercenaries which fought for it could not even clear Greece of the feudal Crusader states which remained there from the Latin conquest. In the early fourteenth century civil war broke out and further sapped the vitality of the state; little remained to oppose effectively the newly risen Serbian power or the ominous encroachments of the Ottomans.

The glory of the Empire in its last days was in the works of the mind and the creative eye. The treasuries of Greek and Hellenistic philosophy which had been stored in East Rome for a millennium were reworked and expounded. New life was infused into Orthodox Christianity, especially through a movement which stressed contemplation and a sort of disciplined mysticism. The Palaeologan mentality was also reflected in its religious art, in lively, rather delicate, brilliantly colored figures. The churches which were dedicated in this period were small—jewelry-work as compared with the great hollow masses of Justinian's triumphant Hagia Sophia or the princely structures of the Macedonians.

Much of the intellectual and artistic achievement of this age was carried to the West. The Palaeologan house had to fulfill its obligation to defend what it held, and the only help was in the West. Embassies were sent, and individual scholars and artists traveled or fled to Italy and beyond, but only a trickle of aid came in return; the suspicious temper of most of the remaining Byzantines was such that negotiations regularly broke down. When the fanatical Ottoman Sultan Mohammed II finally put out his full strength against Constantinople, the Empire's will to live had long been leached away. Siege cannon broke the triple lines of the Long Walls, the last imperial Constantine, eleventh to bear the name, died fighting in the breach, and the Byzantine Empire passed into history.

THE BYZANTINE STATE

The Constitution

The Byzantine conception of the state ruled out any possibility of government by representative democracy, though their knowledge of Greek classical authors gave them knowledge of democracy as well as of all the other modes of ancient government. They probably could not have even conceived of a constitutional or "figurehead" monarchy. There were constituent elements in their state, however, whose agreement—especially at the moment the monarch was chosen—was necessary in order to give legality to the monarch's reign. This is what we will understand by the "Byzantine constitution": those supporting collectives whose agreement, especially *ritual* agreement, made the autocrat legitimate.

SENATE AND PEOPLE

From Rome Byzantium inherited the phrase "Senate and People of Rome" and a shadow of the reality which had once stood behind the phrase. Certainly the Byzantine emperor no longer held to the fiction that he ruled in the name of the Senate and People, i.e., the elders and the mass of citizens. He ruled in God's name, and the new "citizenship" of the Empire was defined not in legal terms, but in terms of *religious* adherence and *cultural* commitment.

Nor was this the only change. The Senate of East Rome even in its palmy days (through the sixth century) was a lineal descendent, not of the Senate of the Roman Republic, of which Cicero had so high an opinion, but of the imperial Senate of later years. Its members were not aristocrats of long lineage, but former civil servants, advanced to the honor of senator after long service. They were "elders," but of the apparatus of the state. Still they held some power—not the power to enact law, but certainly the power or right to advise the emperor, when their advice was asked. The position of senator remained rich in prestige. And it was felt to be proper, to be "constitutional," that the Senate *acclaim* a candidate for the imperial throne even if it did not in fact *name* him. Moreover, in times of emergency, as when an emperor died or was removed without leaving an immediate successor, the Senate could legally rule in the interregnum, thus providing a vital continuity.

Except in these times of emergency, however, the Senate's position was ambiguous and almost anomalous. Powers which it seemed to have held up to the seventh century A.D. it could not keep under the reorganized Empire of that century. Its advisory function passed more and more into the hands of the group of high-ranking administrators who acted as the emperor's consistory, or *Silention.* This group was sometimes called by the name *Synkletos* which had originally meant "Senate." At the very end of the ninth century Leo VI saw fit, as a sort of afterthought, to abridge the old Senate's few remaining privileges, but by that time it certainly had only a ceremonial and an honorary significance.

The People of Rome exercised *their* constitutional role in widely contrasted modes: in ritualized acclamations, by petition (often vocal), and by violence. There was never any doubt in Byzantium that the people had the right to agree or disagree with the acts of their ruler, even when the imperial system was at its stiffest and most autocratic. The emperor, in East Rome, necessarily had an immediate and real relationship with his people, and this puzzles those who think of the emperor only in terms of his unapproachable "divine" status.

The imperial system *did* object to any organization of the people separate from the machinery of state. The spontaneous expression of the people's will might well reflect the will of God, but emperors learned that a grouping, a "party," was dangerous. In the sixth century certain of these parties which had grown out of the cheering sections in the Hippodrome (the great racecourse or circus) grew too powerful and riotous and were put down by force. Thereafter, these factions were given more of a ceremonial significance. Their leaders, the demarchs or "leaders of the People," were closely associated with the palace hierarchy; they were really bureaucrats. This is not to say that they had the job of merely cheer-leading on state occasions, for the ceremonial acclamations by the people were regarded by the Byzantines as vitally important in themselves, like all ceremonies.

The Hippodrome retained its importance, for it was exactly here that people and ruler approached each other; one of the most important confrontations being when a new emperor showed himself in the *kathisma,* or imperial box. The Byzantines centered a great deal of attention on the Hippodrome; they seemed to see in it a simulacrum, an image of the turning world itself. The races, or courses, run there were more than sporting events, they mirrored the cyclical course of human existence, and the powers of fortune as well. Priests, for instance, were forbidden to attend ordinary games, but were allowed to attend the Hippodrome. The great racecourse was an important part of the imperial world, and the emperor could not separate himself from it.

THE CHURCH

The powers of the Orthodox Christian Church, as an influence on the workings of the state, were limited formally to participation in the ceremonies which raised a man to the imperial office. Even in this instance—in the ceremony of coronation—the presence of the patriarch does not seem to have been absolutely necessary. During the doctrinal quarrels of the fifth century, when the emperor's adherence to the true faith was not always certain, a "second coronation" was added to the original crowning, and with this second coronation the patriarch made clear the sanction of the Christian Church. Later a coronation oath was added as well, in which the emperor swore to uphold orthodoxy. However, we know that all these ceremonial additions did not make an emperor legitimate; that had been settled by the fact of his election before the coronation. An emperor could also, without any assistance from the patriarch, raise and crown his own heir apparent.

All of this simply means that the imperial office was not elevated or sanctified in any significant sense by a special "Christian" coronation, because it was *already* a sacred office—the highest. The patriarch, who was by definition a creature of the emperor, only provided the technical approval of the Christian Church organization. God, not the patriarch, chose and anointed the emperor.

The emperor, while ruling, was expected to obey the rules, found in Scripture and the canons, which governed all Christians. He was answerable to all the Christians of the Empire—not to the patriarch, whose organization, which existed in this world, was thereby subordinated to the wide powers of the emperor over worldly things. Occasionally patriarchs tried to extend their role as moral overseer until they came into conflict with the emperor, but these attempts were very seldom successful, and usually cost the ambitious church leader his job.

THE ARMY

The Byzantine Empire resembled the old Roman Empire in the power which the army assumed in the naming and acclaiming of an emperor. However, this power, which in Old Rome remained at best quasi-constitutional, in the Byzantine Empire appears to have been more regularized. An acclamation, or formal acceptance, by the army was obviously very important to the successful accession of the individual emperor, as its cooperation was vital to his success afterwards. But in Byzantium the practical aspect of the power of the military in a state was subordinated to another idea. The army was conceived to act as an instrument in the hand of Providence in choosing one man as emperor; thereafter, a close tie was recognized, and the emperor proved his fitness for the office by leading the army to victory. This was a continuing, and an important, test of the imperial office.

THEORY AND REALITY

If we look at the separate elements which made up the Byzantine body politic for any evidence of formalized controls over the imperial office, we look in vain. We see that the agreement of such groups as the army, the senate, and the church was required at the moment an emperor was chosen. Even at this moment, however, these groups acted not as elective bodies in a political sense but as instruments of the divine will. And, once the emperor was elevated to the throne, no earthly power, not even the church, had a legitimate or constitutional means of questioning his acts.

Naturally the emperor had to depend on his armed forces and his administrators for loyal cooperation. Even here, however, the natural tendency of professional corps to develop their own patterns of action was curtailed. The imperial bureaus, for example, operated under the assumption that the autocrat could at any time circumvent their normal procedures—their "channels"—and work his own will. From the seventh century, in fact, the pyramidal structure which we would expect to find in a highly complex and articulated administrative system was not to be found in Byzantium. Every official, in theory, was responsible to the emperor himself. A system of subordination inevitably was retained, and there had to be officials whose usefulness, and responsibilities, were greater; these made up the *Silention,* or cabinet. The theory was still plain; the Byzantine constitution described the governance of the empire in terms of one man.

The Imperial Office

THEORIES

Was the emperor, in fact, only a man with great power? At first glance the Byzantine conception of the imperial leader appears to offer the most extreme instance of the idea of "divine right." The emperor was, of course, emperor "by the Grace of God." More than this, God's grace made him "holy" (*agios:* literally, "sainted"); "divine"; the "sun on earth." He was "equal to the Apostles," the "God-resembling Emperor," and "a god on earth." These were not merely high-flown ceremonial phrases; they reflected the very real Byzantine belief that it was possible for God to choose as his instrument a man whose powers then became divine powers.

Ostensibly the Byzantine conception of imperial power is merely a Christian extension of the change in, and strengthening of, the imperial idea which took place under the pagan emperors Aurelian and Diocletian (late third century A.D.). These emperors had moved to strengthen their position by making explicit religious sanctions which up to that time had been more understood than formally proclaimed in Rome—by naming themselves "living gods," by associating themselves with the cult of the sun (as an abstract creative power) through the kingly diadem and other regalia, by demanding such ceremonial as the *proskynesis* or extreme genuflection which emphasized their godlike majesty. Yet the acceptance of Christianity did not actually continue this trend toward making a man—the emperor—divine. Christianity—both East and West—did not see the possibility of a man's advancing up a ladder of power to the divine; they saw the divine descending to fill a man's human shell and appearance. No man could affect or bring down on himself God's power. There always remained a difference in kind between man the fallible and God the infallible; this difference became especially visible when the hand of God deserted an emperor, when he suddenly lost the aid of Providence and became a mere man again.

Obviously, then, the emperor's divinely-given right to rule brought both advantages and disadvantages. The Byzantine rulers never became involved in anything resembling the Investiture Controversy in the medieval Western Empire—in any clash of church and state—because the emperor had been from the first much more than merely a political figure. The Byzantines' chief difficulty was to devise some human control over an office which was divine in nature. This difficulty became especially serious when the imperial throne had to be passed from one man to his successor (see p. 40), for here man's choice might be blasphemously opposed to that of God. The fact that the imperial office was thought of in such lofty terms involved it in theological and philosophical speculations which invested it with great power, but which also made certain practical, necessary administrative procedures very troublesome.

THE VICAR OF CHRIST AND THE MIMESIS OF CHRIST

Just how seriously the Byzantines took their imperial masters is plain when we look at another idea which emerges in their "political" theory. This is the idea that the emperor, both in his actions and in his essence—in being and in doing—was the image, or *icon,* of Christ. That one man could play the efficient role of God (as Byzantine "divine right" theory states) and of the Son of God, too, was not at all improbable to the East Romans. Their theology was essentially Christ-centered; they tended to confuse or combine the first two persons of the Trinity until, as we see below, they gave the form of Christ to God, calling the result *Christ Pantokrator,* the All-Ruler, or Judge. An emperor, therefore, could easily reflect both aspects of one deity in his character of Christ-figure.

The Byzantine emperor *was* a Christ-figure; he was not merely the vicar or vicegerent of Christ, ruling in his name, but the true imitation or *mimesis* of Christ—a living image. As such he was expected to perform the same functions that Christ performed: to pass down to his people *philanthropia,* which is love of mankind, and to pass up to the Godhead *eusebeia*—piety of a special kind. This dual and simultaneous function again reduced the emperor to an instrument in divine hands. His love of mankind was not truly his own, but that of Christ reflected through him. His piety was not personal but a focusing of the piety of the nation, or of all nations.

The emperor was thus caught up in the web that the

Byzantines loved to weave: the puzzle of man and God, and of God in man. The power he wielded was immense and apparently unrestricted, but it was not properly his. Here, as elsewhere, the Byzantines distrusted the human and placed their hopes in the supernatural.

THE EMPEROR'S FUNCTIONS

When we see the size of the task an emperor undertook when he mounted the throne of East Rome, we can see how the Byzantines might feel that only God himself could expect to do all that had to be done. An emperor's jurisdiction extended everywhere in theory, for on him devolved the full responsibility for the survival and vitality of the God-given empire, i.e., of the world itself. He held ultimate responsibility for the cure of his subjects' souls and the economic well-being of both the individual and the state. He held all the strings of the complicated Byzantine foreign policy in his hands, and when diplomacy failed, he was expected to take the field with the army, navy, or both. He directed the dominant, twinned Byzantine institutions of ceremony and law, which are important enough to be treated separately below. He had a great deal of assistance from the bureaucracy, but it must be remembered that in theory the emperor knew about, and could interrupt and reverse, any bureaucrat's decision.

1. The discussion of the emperor's function in what we would call the "church" properly belongs below (p. 63). Briefly, the accepted, or Orthodox, faith was a prerequisite for citizenship, or membership, in the empire, and the ruler was its guardian. He could raise or degrade anyone in any

rank of the church hierarchy. As the highest administrator in spiritual affairs, he called and oversaw the councils of the church. Finally, he had a strong, if informal, voice in the shaping of dogma—all in the interest of the realm.

2. The economic base of the Empire remained agricultural, and here the emperor obviously could not guide every detail. He did interest himself in problems of land tenure, as in the settlement of the theme soldiery and the protection of their holdings, and in the vital matter of taxation. The industry and trade of the Empire, especially that located in Constantinople, *was* closely supervised. Items which the state regarded as "strategic" were surrounded by a fence of regulation, enforced by the prefect, or chief officer of the city. The emperor was also in a position to affect the entire economy of the Empire through his control of coinage and the mints. The point to be made is that the emperor had a great deal of the economic life of the Byzantines in his care, and this is occasionally made dramatically clear by such actions as the sequestering of the estates of men whose wealth was too obviously excessive.

3. Direction of the external relations of the state involved the autocrat in a ceaseless round of ceremonial receptions and processions, by which foreign ambassadors were impressed, indoctrinated, and drawn into the orbit of the Empire. The emperor was the director, too, of the great Byzantine diplomatic corps, and he drew the broad outlines of policy which guided them—himself guided by tradition and the eternal patience of the Empire. Our best surviving evidence of this is the admirable work, *On the Administration of the Empire,* addressed to his son by the Emperor Constantine VII. Here, and in such sources as the formularies which regulated imperial diplomatic corre-

spondence, we see that the Byzantines had a picture of a world with the emperor at the center; all other princes were ranked around him. All Christian nations were theoretically subject to him. For the rest (with the possible exception of Persia, when it still existed) the emperor represented the majesty of Christian Rome, of the everlasting idea of ordered power here and hereafter. No barbarian could afford to ignore him, for he had the power to be a generous friend and an implacable enemy. This was a brilliant conceit, and one with surprisingly great strength, even in the declining days of the Empire.

4. When the Byzantines put forth all their military strength the emperor's presence was imperative; his leadership was as necessary as were the great sacred banners. Whether he was a trained soldier or not was by the way. Some emperors were great generals: Maurice and Heraclius, Constantine V, John Tzimiskes and Nicephorus II, Basil II, John Comnenus. Others were inept or unfortunate–like Nicephorus I, originally a bureaucrat, who was killed by the Bulgars, or Romanus IV, captured at Manzikert, or the last Palaeologos–but the trial might come to any who wore the crown. The important thing was not their training or generalship, but victory. The *eusebeia,* piety, of the emperor was tested in battle; he offered himself up. Providence gave him victory or defeat according to his deserts and the ordained destiny of the Empire.

The above is only a sketch of the emperor's most significant functions. The Byzantines would not differentiate between the value of one and the value of the others; all were vitally important. Each emperor fulfilled his functions as best he could; thus, the order of the world was continued.

THE PROBLEM OF SUCCESSION

The Byzantine prejudice against formalizing and institutionalizing the process for passing on imperial power was so marked that it is difficult to see how it was ever done successfully. The statistics are no comfort. In the more than 1000 years between 395 and 1453, 65 emperors were dethroned by force and 41 of these died violently during, or following, the coup which overthrew them; only 39 emperors passed peacefully from the scene. How could the members of one family, like the Macedonians, hold the imperial office for so long in the face of such a record? They managed, obviously, but not through the exercise of a truly dynastic principle. The Byzantines had only a rudimentary theory of dynastic succession, for all their instincts were against it, but other means were found to secure a peaceful transmission of power—sometimes.

Even the most powerful and well-established imperial houses had to contend with the strong Byzantine conviction that the emperor was literally named and his powers confirmed by God. What the Creator gave he could also take away, at his own time and pleasure, and for reasons inscrutable to men. What human arrangement could stand against, or be substituted for, the divine plan? No man could possibly know when the divine protection would be withdrawn, the emperor then ceasing to be an instrument and becoming an obstacle; and the result was a serious weakness at the heart of the imperial system. The continued potency of the reigning autocrat came to be surrounded by a fog of superstitions: belief in prodigies, in "signs," in prophecies made by obscure monks regarding the future success or failure of the ruler. The very insecurity of the throne was institutionalized in Byzantium. Rebellion against God's representative was, of course, the blackest crime, or rather, sin; but the rebellion which succeeded was, equally obviously, the will of God. Only failure was reprehensible. The rebel who failed, deserved to be thrown to the beasts of the arena, but an emperor whose cause failed, was deserving of no more sympathy. Even the *hint* that the reign of the imperial figure was about to be threatened could be enough: it caused the most loyal supporters to withdraw their support, lest they oppose Providence. Threatened emperors themselves often abandoned all hope, and unresistingly gave up their power and their lives.

This was an insidious influence for discontinuity and disintegration; there had to be counterforces, and there were. First, the Byzantines did, from time to time, entrust their highest office to members of particular families in turn, and sometimes, as in the cases of the Macedonians and Palaeologi, these families ruled, good and bad, for centuries. In these instances the continued loyalty of the people seems to have grown out of a feeling, or instinct, that the family was somehow specially favored. The Macedonians, again, were forgiven a great deal in the last days of their house; the last of the line, the two pathetic sisters, Zoe and Theodora, held the people's loyalty through one embarrassing crisis after another. However, the people of the Empire were evidently not motivated by a respect for any rightful, "legitimate" Macedonian succession, so much as by respect for the ancient power and luck of the house. Immediately after the Macedonian line failed, the Byzantines reverted to their worst habits; only in the case of the Palaeologi is any vague notion of dynastic legitimacy visible.

The most familiar and effective device for passing on power from emperor to emperor was simply to associate the heir or successor to the throne by naming him co-emperor during the lifetime of his predecessor. The Byzantines had no trouble accepting two, or even more, holders of a theoretically autocratic and indivisible power: if the Godhead could be divided into three, and yet remain whole, so could the divinely sanctioned imperial office. In the absence of a male heir the reigning ruler might adopt one, often marrying the new candidate into the imperial family. Or, if no provision had been made before an emperor's death, his widow might marry a man who would provide what the Byzantine felt was always necessary: a mature head of state, someone who could take up the massive load of imperial responsibilities. The Byzantines disliked regencies; they disliked being ruled by functionaries in the name of an infant or adolescent. An emperor had to actively carry out his obligations in all areas; the name was not enough.

Hierarchy and Bureaucracy

COURT AND UNIVERSE

The Byzantines inherited from Old Rome a vast and convoluted administrative machine, which extended the emperor's will into the most obscure corners of his subjects' lives. The shift of the Empire to the East, and its Christianization, had their effects on the bureaucracy; so did the pressures of a separate "Byzantine" history, thereafter. We can see that the Hellenistic and Christian (or Hellenized Christian) rendition of Platonic philosophy, which was so influential in the Byzantine idea of the imperial office, also affected their concepts of hierarchy and bureaucracy.

It is always dangerous to talk about the "Orientalization" of Byzantium, for this phrase brings up more problems than it solves, but there *is* evidence of influence from the Persian court. Exactly how this came about we are not sure, but after the collapse of Persia the whole flavor and style of the newly "Byzantine" court seems to become more majestic, more prismatic and measured. We have positive evidence, as well, of court costumes specifically called "Persian." Another influence on the court came out of the progressive militarization of the Empire in the face of the Persian and Arab threat, also beginning in the perilous seventh century, which is reflected in the number of dignities (nonfunctional titles) with a military connotation, such as "Soldier" or "Guardsman," appearing around this time.

From these diverse elements the Byzantines created a court and a bureaucracy: a hierarchic court surrounding the throne in a conscious imaging of universal hierarchy and order, and a functional bureaucracy which ran the Empire. Now, that an administrator should have both a rank and a job is not unfamiliar to us. Our civil servant has a rank or grade (G–3, let us say) and a job (clerk-typist); or, to use an example slightly closer to Byzantine usage, a major general may be Chief of Army Engineers. This is not quite what the Byzantines had in mind. First of all, the honorary grades or dignities were not connected to any job or function at all; only to the emperor. Differenced by type and color, the insignia which distinguished each was in the emperor's gift, from the diploma, which was the sign of the lowest; to the crown without cross, for the highest (the

Caesar: usually the heir apparent). Each insignia admitted its bearer to a particular place in the great cycle of ceremonial, the large and small ceremonies—especially the processions—which both reflected and re-established order in the universe. What the Byzantines seemed to see in ritual and ceremonial was so important to them that it deserves a separate treatment. The point to be made here is that the development of a retinue or court served a special purpose, essentially different from the functional aspect of administering the realm.

Naturally, this was an organic development stretching over centuries, and complete consistency is impossible to find. Included in the table of ranks, for example, was a distinct series—the "Senatorial"—composed of titles from the older Empire which had once been functional. These included "consul" and "proconsul" (Greek *hypatos* and *anthypatos*). There was also a high rank, *magistros,* or master, which had once been limited to the most exalted military and civil officers of the old bureaucracy. An element of confusion is added, because certain minor functionaries who appear in a number of bureaus were designated by their low dignitary rank, *mandator,* once a sort of low-level escort. Translations and transliterations from Latin into Greek also cloud the picture.

One of the most important and significant features of the table of ranks was the use made of it in international relations. The emperor could, and did, grant dignities to foreign rulers or their representatives, usually the rank of patrician or magister. This granting of rank was not only a friendly gesture, for if a foreign prince was included in the ceremonial hierarchy, he was also included in the Empire. The court, to the Byzantine, had a double analogy: first, to the broader Empire with its ranks of peoples and classes surrounding the earthly all-ruler; second, to the eternal, universal economy, where all created things surrounded the central power of God.

It was inevitable that the Byzantines should extend their image of the Christ-imitating emperor to the ranks of dignitaries whom the emperor, informed by grace, had created. Their pattern was the neo-Platonic succession of beings descending from the Godhead. It has been suggested, in fact, that the special corps of eunuchs who acted as body servants to the imperial family (though there were excellent practical reasons for using them) prefigured on earth the sexless choir of angels who served the throne of heaven. To the Byzantines, obviously, the Image was everything; it was a central obsession of their civilization.

THE MACHINERY OF EMPIRE

The Byzantine bureaucracy, whose members were also participants in the court, owed much to Rome: not least, the idea of bureaucracy, of administrative service itself. But the "Roman" emphasis in East Roman administrative procedures had begun to degenerate by the end of the sixth century; and a new structure appeared, somewhat masked by old names. The old Roman imperial administration, first, was severely pyramidal in plan. The large subdivisions of government—finances, the chancery, the courts, the special bureaus—were grouped under two great ministers, the Master of Offices and the Praetorian Prefect. During and after the pivotal seventh century, which we have repeatedly recognized as the first "Byzantine" century, the old superministries disappeared. The theory and structure of pyramidal responsibility and subordination were replaced by a system of greatly expanded *direct* responsibility to the emperor himself. In the fully articulated system at the height of the Empire's power more than 60 bureau chiefs, whose bureaus handled every aspect of government, answered (in theory) directly to the throne.

We have no room (and no necessity) to list all the bureaucrats of East Rome and their various functions—when these functions are clear to us at all. There were, however, a small number of officials of particular usefulness to the Empire, whose jobs are worth examining, not least because they show what functions the Byzantines *did* think particularly useful. We have clues to their importance in the historical sources, in the prominent positions they held in the protocol-dominated state dinners, in ceremonies, and through the evidence of outside observers (especially Arab travelers or prisoners, and some Westerners). They include two officials with extensive legal powers (prefect of the city and *quaestor*), three officers of the treasury (*logothetes*), the comptroller (*sakellarios*), the chief secretary, and a civil servant of peculiar origins who was the de facto foreign minister of the realm (logothete of the course).

1. The *prefect of the city* was always ranked high in the Empire, since the administration of the capital city was in his care. His importance as a legal officer came from the size and complexity of his jurisdiction, though he may have had an appellate jurisdiction as well. The *quaestor* had some specialized legal functions, but most of his time seems to have been spent in directing the work of his bureau, which replied to petitions demanding justice from the emperor. If the emperor had any official qualified to advise him on legal questions, it would have been this official.

2. The financial apparatus of the Byzantine state was especially complicated: there were three treasurers, con-

trolling three main subdivisions—taxation, the military chest, and "special accounts." The *sakellarios* exercised a central control. There were, however, monies disbursed and records kept in other departments, such as the Wardrobe and the Department of Imperial Estates.

3. *The chief secretary* (*protoasecretes*) headed the corps of "notaries" who drew up imperial documents connected only with general administration, not financial matters or legal questions.

4. The *logothete of the course* evidently had his origins in the branch of government he would later head: the *Cursus Publicus,* or Public Post. This vital service was the communications link of the Empire; through it the Logothete became involved in diplomatic matters (since all foreign and Byzantine diplomats used the post for transportation, not for letters), until he finally headed all the technical services connected with this area: the corps of interpreters, the post, supply, and so on. The *Logothete* had a considerable ceremonial role in the reception of ambassadors.

Two other highly placed officials might be mentioned: the *rector,* who seems to have supervised the imperial household; and the *synkellos,* who was a civil servant acting as liaison officer between emperor and patriarch.

These eight to ten men, along with two or three prominently placed eunuchs, were the chief civil servants of the realm, during the zenith of Macedonian power. They, and their theoretically equal fellows in slightly less significant posts, commanded an army of lesser bureaucrats, and the long success of the Empire was owing, in great part, to the professionalism of that army. The career of civil servant was traditional and honorable, and it attracted cultured men, in the Byzantine style, for learning was recognized as a prerequisite for both service and advancement. The bureaucracy was an influential element in Byzantine culture, and much of the attractively deliberate and rhythmic quality of Byzantine life—and its conservatism and narrow-mindedness as well—can be traced to the dominance of bureaucratic attitudes. At any rate, for good or ill, the Byzantine state supported its great central figure with a mass of pen-pushers.

Ceremony and Law

THE USES OF CEREMONY

In the prologue to the massive work *On the Court Ceremonies of the Byzantines* by the Emperor Constantine VII, the imperial author gives his reasons for devoting his time to the book. First, the ceremony decorates the Empire, beautifies it, for order and harmony are always beautiful. Second, the ceremony insures that the imperial power is exercised with the rhythm and order which is necessary, so that the Empire will represent its exemplar, the universal harmonious motion which the Creator ordained. The emperor here uses the image of a mirror, which reflects, to all who wish to see, the essential propriety and orderliness of the imperial government.

The Byzantine sense of ritual, and hunger for it, almost evades our imagination. Each component of a particular ceremony held a weight of meaning lost, in great part, to us. The colors of the garments of the imperial family and their retinue were symbolically varied, as were the shapes and forms of regalia and insignia. The inclusion of a particular corps of dignitaries, or their place in procession or audience hall, had meaning; so did the presence or absence of certain pieces of ceremonial furniture at the state dinners. The music and musicians seem to have been extraordinarily varied, though the Byzantines depended a good deal on those two most evocative instruments, the organ and the human voice. The people as spectators, where the ceremonies took place outside the Sacred Palace, were injected into the course of the ceremony by their repetitive shouts of acclamation. Finally, we can only guess at the cumulative effect: the aura of age and tradition, the strong religious feeling, the pressure and surge of timeless power, the sense that each ceremony was part of a chain which led into the Infinite.

As a stage for these rituals, the city itself was a valuable asset, but within the capital were special focuses for the most significant events. Grouped on the acropolis at the tip of the city's peninsula was the Hippodrome, the great cathedral of Hagia Sophia, and the Sacred Palace, each with its own import in the ceremonial cycle. Of the three, the Sacred Palace was the theater in which the most varied dramas were played out. Its plan, so far as we can reconstruct it, both served, and was served by, the rituals which pulsed and glowed there.

Begun by the Constantinids, the palace was gradually expanded, until in the tenth century (when Constantine VII collected his ceremonies) it was an ordered jumble of audience halls, porticoes, stairways, guard rooms, great and small dining rooms, churches and chapels, apartments, and areas for recreation. Its size, the richness of construction and furnishings, and the pattern of the whole reflected the Byzantine ideal of regularized variation and the eventual harmony of distinct notes.

Using the Sacred Palace as a mechanism, the Byzantines could expose guests, such as certain Saracen envoys in the tenth century, to a polychromatic display of Imperial pomp. The Saracens, we are told, entered the great ceremonial gate called Chalkè (the Copper Gate). They waited near the magnificent buildings housing the Household Regiments while the emperor passed before them with his retinue and entered the Magnaura palace where audiences were held. They followed "into the Metatorion of the Great Triclinium of the Magnaura," escorted by "the Catepan of the Basilics and the Count of the Stables." After ritualized greetings and the ceremony of audience they left, passing through "the Vine-Room . . . the Triclinium of the Candidati . . . the Triclinium in which the Kamelaukion [a sort of canopy] stands . . . through the Onopous and the Portico of the Augusteia called the Golden Hand . . . into the Triclinium of the Augusteus . . ." Each of these names had, to the Byzantines, a resonance and a power; they immediately identified a particular fragment of the physical setting for ceremony.

The emperor then passed with all his retinue in procession and went on into the depths of the palace; the Saracens followed

> . . . through the Diabatikon and the Apse into the Covered Hippodrome as far as the Skyla [Gate], and having come in were seated in the western part of the Triclinium of Justinian II on small couches.

After a state dinner, accompanied by music and with munificent gifts presented at the end, these Saracen envoys were conducted out of the palace by another route, leaving by a smaller gate rather than by the Chalkè by which they had entered.

This description gives some idea of the physical grandeur of the palace setting; we are likely to be impressed even at this distance, though we can see only a shadow of what surrounded the Saracens. Like the German Bishop Luitprand, who gaped at the hydraulic throne of Solomon and the mechanical singing birds and roaring lions in the Magnaura, we see an old civilization putting on an excellent show. The Byzantines surely enjoyed magnificence, but their ceremonial was much more than this. It was, strictly speaking, a series of "liturgies," in the original meaning of the word—something which had to be done. The carefully planned and meticulously executed processions—the Byzantines attached special meaning to movement—mimicked the procession of all the ranks of created beings, the movements of the universe. The motion of the universe was eternal, and to mirror and recreate it ensured the Empire's eternal life.

Byzantine ceremonial, then, was not a show, a series of impressive cynical performances to captivate the heathen visitor or the poor of the city. Nor was it only "play," though it certainly gratified all the Byzantine feeling for well-organized assaults on the senses; the feeling for color and rhythm, brilliance, visible power, and awesome display. Byzantine ceremonial was necessary because it imaged that organization which all the world, seen and unseen, shows, and, because in reflecting and representing, it *continued* that harmony; it "drew the world on." There was no essential difference between the sacred and the secular ceremony; the personnel might change, but the high purpose was the same. Constantine's *Book of Ceremonies* does reveal several distinct types: the court ceremonies which followed the sacred cycle of Christian feasts; the high secular ceremonies celebrating the greatest imperial events of coronation, marriage, birth, baptism, and the installation of all the ranks of dignitaries. There are rituals which were only of antiquarian interest to Constantine himself, and others which interest us because they decorated certain historically significant occasions. In each, the same idea is clear: The multiform ritual, through the senses, leads the mind to perceive the eternal Creation.

LAW AND ORDER

THE EMPEROR IN LAW

Law, to the Byzantines, drew its essence from the same source as ceremonial, for it reflected the divine order of the universe. In the case of law, however, the role of the emperor, who directed the recreation of order in both instances, shifted upward. In his legal role the emperor was more philanthropic, i.e., Godlike, and less pious. His Type or model was Christ the Judge.

Roman tradition, and what we call Roman law, had made Caesar the highest judge. (Roman law today maintains its emphasis on the judge.) Christian influences elevated Caesar still higher, and in the Byzantine Empire he was not only the highest judge and the maker of law but the "living law," the source of that divine justice which is above, and incomprehensible to, the laws and minds of men. The emperor, then, while he fitted the pattern of life—the laws governing the acts of men—to the eternal model, could interrupt that pattern to bring about a higher justice; he could perform his own "miracles." These miracles would be, ordinarily, acts of mercy and *philanthropia*.

At the same time that the Byzantines recognized the emperor as having great power in, and even above, the law, they also recognized authorities independent of him—authorities to which the emperor was expected to turn for guidance. These included Scripture and canon law, and also "custom sanctified by age." At least one imperial code even mentions the old classical formula of moderation, "nothing too much," as a desirable feature in law. The point is that even though the Byzantines believed in a systematized, man-made law, they were not convinced that men could ever do more than approximate the higher Law. Justice was ultimately in God's hands.

THE LAW CODE

With all their reservations, the Byzantines still were responsible for the primary Roman codes of law from which a long Western tradition springs. A collection and tabulation of laws—that is to say, imperial edicts—was issued under the name of the Emperor Theodosius in the fifth century, but the Code of Justinian, a century later, was a more comprehensive and significant attempt. This great code was part of Justinian's formula for renovating the Roman world, but even before its completion, its usefulness was limited in the Greek-speaking East. The last section, Justinian's own *Novels* or new laws, was necessarily in Greek; the other sections—the Code proper, the *Digest* (of jurists' opinions), and the *Institutes* (a textbook for students of law)—were in Latin.

Whatever its linguistic drawbacks, the Code of Justinian was the nearest thing to an immutable positive Law that the Byzantines recognized. It was never really superseded. Translations and handbooks based on it were used until the Isaurian period, when Leo III and his son issued their manual, the *Ekloga*, "with a view toward greater humanity." This humaneness seems to consist in the substitution of other penalties, especially mutilation, for death; some experts have seen an "Oriental" tinge to the *Ekloga.* It remained in force until the Macedonians appeared; Basil I and his son Leo VI then issued a handbook and later a complete code, the *Basilics,* which was modeled on Justinian's original work. Though some forms and procedures would change thereafter, the *Basilics* remained in force until the end of the Empire.

The edicts, or laws-by-decree, of individual emperors were expected to be in the spirit of the prevailing code. As a matter of fact, the great majority of imperial edicts were procedural rather than substantial, and were aimed at the magistrates of the realm. Concretely, justice was in their hands, and as the social fabric of the Empire began to disintegrate the principles of the great law codes became less and less pertinent. (Justice, the ideal and the actuality, had slipped from the emperor's hands.)

BYZANTINE CHRISTIANITY

Historical Sketch

"Byzantine Christianity" is used here to mean a particular Christian formation, chronologically separate from, but rooted in, the more or less unified Christian doctrinal structure of the fourth–sixth centuries and separate from the Western Church. Byzantine Christianity is not what we now call Eastern Orthodoxy either, although the Eastern Orthodox churches are consciously rooted in the Byzantine past and continue many of the dogmatic and liturgical emphases of the Church of East Rome.

Byzantine Christianity took the form it did because of two major influences: (a) the theological explorations and controversies of the eastern part of Christendom, and (b), the close ties binding the church to the imperial office and the imperial idea. The first influence gave a particular bias to Byzantine spirituality, for the Byzantines followed the great theologians called "Alexandrian," and their disciples, in emphasizing the spirit behind the word, the mystical rather than the historical element in Christianity. The second influence kept the church from having an isolated development, for the "church"—the organization—was only one of the hierarchy of earthly organizations over which the emperor ruled. The crises which marked the history of Byzantine Christianity usually came when the emperor acted to bring the church into harmony with the rest of the Empire, which, as chief administrator, he was occasionally forced to do.

These crises included the "Monophysitic" controversy of the fifth to seventh centuries, when one imperial compromise after another failed to quiet the Eastern Christians. Another was the movement called iconoclasm in the eighth and ninth centuries, when the acts of the iconoclastic emperors forced radical, and ultimately unacceptable, changes of doctrine on their subjects. Certainly there were gradual evolutionary shifts of belief on the part of the mass of Byzantines which the emperors could not deflect; for example, the growing antagonism to Latin Christianity. Even the reborn Byzantine mysticism of the fourteenth century had its political dimension and became embroiled in political causes. What is clear from all this is that the history of the *structure* of the church did not really concern the Byzantines. To them the operative concept was not church or organization but *oecumene*—the body of all Christians—a loosely defined, inclusive idea which often was simply substituted for "Empire."

Basic Assumptions and Dogma

GOD AND MAN

Byzantium accepted the New Testament's declaration that all men were equal under God. As a matter of fact, Byzantium went further in recognizing the fundamental equality of all Christians than did other Christian cultures. No essential division, for example, was raised between cleric and layman; no additional sanctity was granted the priest because of his office or function. Both priest and layman were sinners; both shared the same hope of salvation.

East Rome's problems were of another sort. They arose particularly out of the welter of complex theological constructions produced in the fourth and fifth centuries, when Christianity subjected its own body of revealed truths to the philosophers—to the rational mind of man. Grave questions were asked, such as: If there *is* something of the divine in man, how much is there? Is there an unbridgeable gap between the nature of God and that of man? Or, if this gap can be bridged, does man have the power to do it? To put the question another way: How is it possible to know God at all? Can He be known in this life, but more important, how will man know Him after death? How can man be saved?

These questions are inescapable in all forms of Christianity, and are encountered in other religions as well. In Christianity they are caught up in a second enigma, the explanation of the nature of *the* Man, of Jesus Christ's human and divine qualities. If we put this problem aside for a moment, and look for the answers the Byzantines provided for the first set of questions, we will see that although they were not completely consistent, there is a suggestion of a pattern to be seen.

In the first place, the divine in man was a mystery, and it remained a mystery. Christians were assured that they, like Christ, had God in them. Unaided, however, they could not put their humanity aside completely. The divine flowed into man from above; the active principle was and remained outside man, though man could try to expose himself to it.

The Byzantines could not rid themselves of the consciousness of the chasm between the human and the superhuman. Moreover, they lived in a state of perpetual anxiety over the further question of whether or not God really intended to admit mankind to salvation at all. The promise had been made, and supposedly the drama of the human passion of Christ supported that promise. Yet the Byzantines tended to push aside the human aspect or nature of Christ, and emphasize his Godhead. The fact that man had been chosen as a vehicle for Incarnation was less important to them than the awesomeness of the *fact* of Incarnation itself, the descent of a transcendent God. When the humanity of Christ fades, the vision of the Old Testament God-as-Judge returns. Supposedly, man is to be lifted up, but will he be? Only an omnipotent and omniscient God knew, and the Byzantines alternated between fear and hope.

Fortunately there were means whereby salvation might be approximated or temporarily reproduced. Direct experience of the divine mysteries *was* possible, through the sacramental event or the liturgy, and through asceticism—the disciplining or conditioning of body and mind to receive God. The Byzantine emphasis on these two methods was very important, for through them, the Christian believer might break the bonds of time and exist in eternity.

As far as human *reason* was concerned, the Byzantine approach was to respect it, but limit it. The Byzantines accepted theology—the logical explication of revealed or nonlogical truths—but stressed the inability of reason or logic to penetrate beyond a certain barrier into the vast unknowableness of God. This position is not uncommon in Christianity, where such a strange combination of history and mystery is always apparent, but the Byzantines rated man's rational powers even lower than most Christians did or do now. East Rome was not fertile ground for scientific theologians. The Byzantines took the strongly mystical, spiritual theologies of the Alexandrians of the fourth and fifth centuries, and submitted them to John of Damascus for final formulation in the seventh century. A balanced amount of Greek Platonist and Aristotelian philosophy was received into the canon at that time—Platonist in its view of transcendent Godhead; Aristotelian in the thoroughness and rational intricacy of John's organization, his "fixed, clear, precise exposition of revealed truths." Very little would be done to amend John's structure in the centuries which followed. His theology would become part of the accepted tradition, like the formulae of the Seven Church Councils, or the "golden-tongued" sermons of Saint John Chrysostom.

There remained the problem of man and sin. The Byzantine idea of sin was affected by Platonist doctrines, which denied that there could be such a thing as positive evil. "Evil" was a lack or loss of "good," and this was translated into Christian terms so that sin became a diminution of the divine in man. This relieved the Byzantines of any overdependence on mechanisms for rebalancing accounts, like the system of penances in the West, once a sin had been committed, but it also reduced man's active part in his relationship to God. The elimination of sin—the "deification" of man—remained in God's hands. The sinner had to depend on the Almighty's "love of mankind" (*philanthropia*) as he depended on the earthly emperor's "love of his subjects" (*philanthropia*). This "love of mankind" was specifically defined as an attribute of power; it was a father's love, if it could be spoken of in human terms at all.

THE VITAL CHRISTOLOGY

The ambiguous nature of the tie between God and man made the Byzantines that much more concerned with the central drama of Christianity, the Incarnation. The puzzle of the descent of God into human flesh fascinated this civilization, and Christology—the explanation of the true nature of Christ—dominated religious thought throughout the life of the Empire. It was paramount in the Monophysitic controversy, it lay behind much of the iconoclastic quarrel, and it vitally affected the full statement of Byzantine Christianity in later centuries.

The Byzantines always were strongly tempted to limit the human aspect of Christ. They reveal this tendency, first, in their suppression of the narrative or historical element in the Gospels. The events of Christ's human life were to be treated as the Alexandrian school of theology directed: as allegories and symbols of the higher drama of salvation. Second, the activity of the "man" in Christ's nature was drastically reduced in significance. According to the compromise position made official at the Council of Chalcedon (451 A.D.), the position which remained "Orthodox," the two natures of Christ were perfect, separate, and contained in one body or appearance. But, as a modern scholar has noted, "Monophysitism was a perpetual temptation to the Christian East." Monophysitism recognized a human appearance—a body or shell—in Christ, but within this shell was very little of man. There was barely enough to make the Passion of Christ meaningful. The Godhead of Christ, however, was always important to the Byzantines.

In large measure the iconoclastic point of view can be interpreted as the logical extension of the Byzantine Monophysitic urge. The icon-breakers wanted to shatter the last remainder of the physical nature of Christ; they wanted no image of this physical appearance to intrude itself between the worshiper and the Worshiped. However, they went too far, for the Byzantines could not tolerate complete isolation from a transcendent divinity. They had to have means for direct contact or communication, and the icon proved to be necessary to them, or to most of them.

The last stage in the Byzantine "divinizing" of Christ can be seen in an iconographic type which first appeared in the ninth century: the *Christ Pantokrator*. The *Pantokrator* or All-Ruler icon was placed in the highest part of the church, in the dome, or in the conch (quarter-sphere) of the apse above the altar. It was literally, as well as symbolically, the loftiest iconic figure. This *Pantokrator* is the First Person in the Trinity in the guise of the Second Person; it is God the Judge, stern or sorrowful, but almighty. Any suggestion that Christ is the intercessor for mankind has all but vanished here.

Other significant iconic themes of the post-iconoclastic period are the Ascension and the so-called *Anastasis*, or harrowing of hell. In the latter, a salient event of the series of feasts celebrated at Easter, Christ was seen by the Byzantines as descending into hell, where he threw down its gates and brought forth the first sinners, Adam and Eve. This, more than the crucifixion or the resurrection of his body, caught the attention of the Byzantines. It is also important to remember that the Byzantines, and the Christian churches of the East who fell into their inheritance, traditionally saw Easter as of more significance than the Nativity. The liberation of Christ from the human form was vastly more vital to them than his appearance on earth.

What all of this points to is a particular view of Christ's nature and mission which reflects directly on the means, and the possibility, of salvation. In this view, Christ is not Man and God at once, and thus at a midpoint between the two, but is so much more God, that man must stand alone. The divine and the human do not complement or assist each other. The lower reaches out as best it can to the higher, but the real efficient force is God's, and man hopes that it will descend to him.

One result of the loss of Christ as interceding power was the elevation of Mary to this position in icon and liturgy. Here again, however, a process of deification is clear; exemplified by the names Virgin and *Theotokos* (Godbearer). Her human life and human attributes are much less apparent in the East than they are, for example, in the Mariolatry of the Roman Catholic West.

The Byzantines, to sum up, received a philosophical heritage which tended to distrust the physical and used it primarily as a lens through which to view the most important Christian drama, that of Incarnation. They reduced the life of the *historical* Christ to a series of symbolic and ritual acts; they reduced his physical nature wherever they encountered it to an absolute minimum, and as far as was possible, they regarded Father and Son as one. The strain which this conception put on man the sinner, they were willing to accept.

STATE AND CHURCH

A number of hints have already been dropped about the refusal of the Byzantines to make the logical (to us, at any rate) separation of the body of the faithful from the body politic—of church from state. This they did refuse to do, but to understand their attitude we must reexamine the emperor's place in the Christian world.

The phrase usually used to describe the Byzantine mode of joining church and state at the top is *Caesaropapism*. The emperor, according to this definition, was both Caesar, or secular monarch, and pope, or absolute head of the church. The term oversimplifies matters considerably. There was no question about the emperor's supremacy in the physical world or body politic, but there were all sorts of ambiguities in his relationship with the church hierarchy, and with the body of all Christians.

Suspicions of Caesaropapism seemed to crop up especially when the Byzantines dealt with the West. Justinian, in his magnificent church at Ravenna, San Vitale, went far in ordering pictorial representations which suggested his own priestly role. The well-known mosaic in the apse places Justinian, symbolically, within the Holy of Holies, eternally bearing his gifts. Moreover, elsewhere in Ravenna there is a mosaic which represents Melchizedek, the archetypal priest-king of the Old Testament, and the figure has Justinian's features. However, we have no idea whether the Ravennese propaganda reflected Justinian's ambitions throughout his Empire or if, as some have suggested, he was using his imperial position to bolster Ravenna at the expense of Rome and Milan, the two important rival centers of Christianity in the West at the time.

In the midst of the iconoclastic furor, in a letter addressed to the pope, Leo III again brought up the spectre of Caesaropapism. For, said Leo bluntly, "I am priest and king." The point may well have been, however, that in dealing with the West, Leo felt that he had to use terms which the West—the pope—would understand. In his own dominions that was not necessary. Leo could simply state there that he was the emperor, and it was immediately understood that he had a function which was quintessentially *religious* if not necessarily priestly.

It is notable that the iconoclastic controversy brought out, in reaction, the strongest protests against the religious role of the emperor: protests which purposefully separated the functions of priest and king. John of Damascus and Theodore of Studium, both zealous icon-worshipers, in turn appealed to the Gospels, to the injunction to render unto Caesar and unto God what belongs to each. This was not, however, the normative point of view.

We have already seen that the emperor, as the animate image of Christ, had a double task which was fundamentally religious. When the emperor's relationship with the patriarch is examined, we find strong evidence that the Byzantines saw no ambiguities at all. The emperor had the responsibility of overseeing the welfare of both the bodies and souls of his subjects; the patriarch looked to their souls only. In the Byzantine view the patriarch was an extremely important clerical figure, one who himself was the icon of Christ as Truth—as the emperor was the icon of Christ as Power. Still, he was *not* the separate head of a church standing away from the state, but the head of an organization fulfilling certain functions. His primary task was to act not in conflict with the emperor, but in what East Rome called *synphonia* with him—in harmony. The patriarch, as the highest priest in the realm, had no more specifically *spiritual* power than did any other priest, and we recall that the Byzantines recognized the difference between layman and priest as being one of function, not kind. Nominated and supported by the emperor, the patriarch enjoyed a certain enhanced jurisdiction, but did *not* have total responsibility for the souls of the people of the nation. The Byzantines actually considered him "crucified to the world," i.e., one who took up the overseeing of an earthly organization at the cost of ignoring the care of his own soul. This picture of the strictly limited powers of the patriarch is not invariably seen in Byzantium, but exceptions were not common.

To the Byzantines, the empire was also, inevitably, the *oecumene*, the Christian world or body of the faithful. East Rome would use this term rather than "church." They expected their church to organize and supervise the details of everyday Christian life, to be the repository of the sacred canon law, to administer, finally, the rituals and sacraments which were a foretaste of salvation. At the same time, there existed at least one other important means to salvation which was actually separate from the church; this was individual asceticism, the total retreat from the world. The monk or ascetic was certainly part of Orthodox Christianity, but his approach to the basic problem of the faith put him apart from the organization.

Special Forms and Emphases

LITURGY AND SACRAMENT

In their view of the power of sacrament and liturgy the Byzantines showed again their intellectual and spiritual ties with the Hellenistic world. The Byzantine belief in the effectiveness of sacraments relates Byzantine Christianity most closely to the whole series of Hellenistic "mystery" cults—most of them, like Christianity, much affected by later forms of Platonist philosophy. Through the repetition of the essential, "sacred-making" events, the Byzantine believer, like his predecessors in other sects, experienced the divine directly. The Byzantines were never much concerned with the precise numbering of the sacraments. They recognized many, with various forms and significances. At the same time, they felt an urgent need to organize and decorate the fabric of the sacred services. To give form to the sacramental occasion, they emerged with a number of liturgies. One, the so-called Liturgy of Saint John Chrysostom, was most commonly used.

Of all the sacraments, the primary, since it enforced the promise of salvation, was the Eucharist. The eucharistic service stood in relation to the other sacraments as Easter did to the rest of the Christian feasts: it was the moment when the most effective instruments for mediating between man and the Divine were brought to bear on the worshiper. The Byzantine service is significantly different from other Christian celebrations of the mystery, for it is not a commemoration, nor an Appearance brought about through the instrumentality of the priest, but an "opening into eternity," an Epiphany of Christ at the Feast of Bride and Bridegroom, in which the Christian in the congregation experiences the actual event of the supper, not as it was, or as it will be, but as it is forever.

The structure of the Byzantine church joined with the form of the liturgy to support this timeless celebration. Though the altar was closed off from the worshipers by the *iconostasis,* the icon screen, the whole interior of the church was sanctified and the faithful with it. The sacrament filled the spherical, hollow spaces which were so necessary to the Byzantines, as figuring on earth the shape of the universe. To increase the effect of the ritual, a variety of elements were brought to bear: numbers of icons with their special meaning; gestures, colors, odors, and sounds which forced all the senses to respond. The congregation was led to a consciousness of symbolic meaning—the true reality behind sense—and to the experience of a double Logos: the Logos, or Grace, which poured down on the communicant, and the Logos, or Word, in the cycle of spoken prayers. Those exposed to this were expected literally to experience heaven.

Another sacrament which was highly regarded was that of baptism. Here the physical act, the contact with water, was surrounded by a web of allegoric and symbolic connections. The central idea of death and rebirth was recalled by the Old Testament figures of Noah and Jonah, who in turn prefigured the baptized Christ. He was the New Adam and New Jonah who conquered death, and was in turn a model for the newly admitted Christian, whose soul rose from death like Lazarus or, like a fish, swam in the Water of Life.

The sacramentary emphasis of the Byzantine church was strongly supported by the cult of icons and of relics, as these beliefs finally emerged, and presented that combination of the physical and the transcendental which was irrevocably fixed in Byzantine civilization. The liturgies followed the same pattern. An extraordinary burst of activity and inventiveness in the fifth and sixth centuries set the liturgical mode for the East Romans, a mode filled in and reinforced later by the hymn-writers. The liturgical year, beginning on the same date as the secular year (September 1), was divided into three main sections, of which the most important was the pre-Easter cycle. On individual occasions within these cycles the Byzantines could draw on an immense and growing fund of meaningful words, spoken or set to music, and actions. Again, their aim was to appeal both to the senses and through them, to the perceiving mind. They seem to have succeeded. The massive weight of Byzantine church ritual, to which some of the best minds of the Empire contributed, was (with the great rituals of state) a potent act of civilization.

MONASTIC IDEALS

At all times the possibility of withdrawing from the world stayed with the Byzantines as a permanent temptation. East Roman Christianity saw two roads to salvation (or rather, roads by which salvation might come). One road was for every Christian who experienced the sacraments and the liturgy; one was for the elect who went beyond, to a life of spiritual discipline, contemplation, and prayer in the monastery. The power which guardianship of the sacraments gave to the Byzantine priesthood was never as great as the power which the monks, the Christian elect, wielded. The monks were felt to be outside the church as organization, and it was suspected (by the iconoclastic emperors, for example) that they felt themselves to be outside the Empire, as well.

Byzantine monasticism came out of the same ground as Christian monasticism generally, but in its essentials it remained close to the classical mode formed in the fourth to sixth centuries. The extreme solitary discipline practiced in Egypt was moderated, though it always remained as a desirable goal; communities of monks became the norm, devoted mostly to work and prayer. Few became priests, only as many as were necessary to conduct sacred services in the monasteries. Byzantine monks never separated into orders, as in the West, but remained under one rule or set of regulations: that of Saint Basil, which counseled poverty, chastity, obedience, and manual labor. They kept two characteristics: they had more mobility than we would usually credit monks with having; despite this, they tended to concern themselves very little with the life of the community at large; they neither preached nor taught, or seldom.

The relationship of the monastic community to the Byzantine church organization was definitely one of superior to inferior in Byzantine eyes. This was an attitude a number of emperors would have liked to reverse, but they had no success. Monastic life affected and influenced the lesser Christian institution. All of the higher ranks of the church hierarchy were drawn from the regular or monastic clergy, and a number of ritual and liturgical practices originated in the monasteries, and were passed on from there to the rest of the Christian community.

The separate status of the monks is nowhere better seen than in the iconoclastic crisis, when the monasteries were the focal point of opposition to iconoclasm. The most brilliant defender of icon-worship was Theodore, abbot of the monastery of Studium, and most monks were as zealously, if not as intellectually, committed to the fight against the imperial will. The partial victory of icon-worship reinforced the stature of Byzantine monasticism, which would be challenged later on economic, but rarely on dogmatic, grounds. Byzantine monasticism has been called, and with reason, a republic within the state, a republic which emperors themselves often aided.

The lure of the unadulterated Christian life, the life devoted to the pursuit of the assurance of salvation, was a powerful one. In theory, the monk, having withdrawn from the secular world, was in an ideal position to take the next step: the cultivation of a contemplative discipline (*ascesis*, whence the name *ascetic*) which would let the Godhead flow into him as into a vessel emptied of sense and thought. Few went so far. Byzantine monasticism developed its own restrictions on the individual: the repetition of liturgy, the substitution of communal prayer for solitary contemplation. With this, unlike the medieval monasticism of the West, it tended to distrust the mind and intellectualizing. Theodore of Studium was an exceptional monk; East Roman intellectual traditions were kept up by other groups and were maintained in the secular world, although monkish chroniclers recorded a sort of "history."

BYZANTINE MYSTICISM

The Byzantine search for individual, transcendent religious experience—a mystical knowledge of the Godhead—moved, by definition, away from the sacramental and toward the monastic or ascetic ideal. The peculiar character of Byzantine mysticism was its limitation and stabilization, the result of a strong dependence on a particular theological, actually philosophical, formula.

Its texts were provided by the two Cappadocian saints, Gregory of Nazianzen and Gregory of Nyssa, and the fourth-century mystic who called himself Dionysius the Areopagite. Dionysius had fitted the personal mystical experience into the cosmic structure described by Neo-Platonic philosophy, and Byzantine mystics tended to hold to the closely formulated limitation of man's reason contained therein. Byzantium did not produce the rich range of Christ-centered mystics which the medieval West boasted —the men "seized by Christ," or the women whose descriptions of their ecstasies in the mystic union with the Godhead suggested heresy at the time, and sexual fantasy now.

Byzantium's explorers of this type of religious experience tended to be mystical thinkers rather than mystics. The two most influential, Maximus the Confessor in the seventh century and Gregory Palamas in the fourteenth, resemble one another in their similarly strong Neo-Platonist leanings and in the fact that both came to oppose the "political" church organization. Maximus, who explicated and passed on the writings of the two Gregorys and Dionysius, ended his life in exile because he stood against both patriarch and emperor in their attempt to find a middle way between orthodoxy and Monophysitism. Gregory Palamas and the movement called Hesychasm (from *hesychia:* silence, contemplative quiet) which emerged in the last days of the Empire, faced a similar sort of opposition.

In the fourteenth century certain doctrines which extended the old ideas of contemplative *hesychia* arrived in the Empire. According to these ideas, which much resemble similar teachings in both Buddhism and Brahmanism, it was possible to achieve a vision of the Divine Light by assuming a set position and repeating the so-called "Jesus prayer." A quarrel immediately blew up over this practice and the theological contentions behind it, in which the Hesychasts were opposed by the more orthodox, philosophically oriented scholars of court and church.

The chief defender of Hesychasm was Gregory Palamas, a monk who set out to prove that the Divine Light experienced by the Hesychasts was a true emanation, a part of the energy of God. To prove this he struck at the idea that human reason could ever penetrate to the Godhead unaided. Yet some contact had to come about, or man was lost. Palamas was, in fact, ridden by the old Byzantine urge to provide some bridge between God and man, a bridge which the Byzantines consistently denied could be constructed by men's minds. For all its trimming of practices which resemble yoga, Hesychasm went back to roots deep in East Rome, growing out of the Christian emphasis on divine revelation, and long nourished by the neo-Platonist theories of a transcendent Godhead made known through mystical experience.

The gap which the concentration on mystery (whether aided by the physical, as in the case of sacrament or completely divorced from the physical, as in the case of individual mystical contemplation) left in the Byzantine religious sense is a large and obvious one. The Byzantines lacked an everyday ethical consciousness. Byzantine Christianity concerned itself very little with the ethical aspects of religion; its sermons, for example, had a strong leaning toward theological elaborations—often with great style, subtlety, and beauty of language, to be sure. Like the later Calvinists, the Byzantine image of a perfectly transcendent God severely limited for them any possibility of man's free will. Unlike the Calvinists, however, they developed no moral system which operated as an assurance that the morally pure were in fact chosen and saved. This is not to say that there were not moral men in Byzantium, but the *tone* of the civilization was set by imperatives other than a fully worked-out ethical system.

THE BYZANTINE MIND

Exactly how the Byzantines looked at their world is not easily discovered. We can make, and we have made, generalizations and approximations; much of their thought is fully recoverable, with a little effort, and perhaps the most cloudy and enigmatic of their patterns of thought and attitude have been marked off and set aside. Examining certain fundamental institutions, and tracing the history of the Empire, we have encountered hints, certainly, of a specifically Byzantine mentality at work. Now there remains the job of defining that mentality more strictly, if we can.

There are three strands or strains which emerge so often in the history and life of East Rome that they cannot be avoided. They are (1) a dependence on the theory of the icon, in all its forms; (2) a combination of a pragmatic, common-sense attitude with a vast unconcern for the affairs of the world—in other words, a perceptible tension between practicality and impracticality; (3) a strong inclination to deny time, in our reading of the term, and history as we would define it.

The Icon

THE IDEA OF THE ICON

The Greek word *eikon* or image was given in Byzantium a special significance. To the Byzantines the icon was the physical memorandum of something beyond; the window (the term is often used) through which men may look into higher realms, and through which in return the divine Word-and-Light flows down from the Creator. The icon was one of the Byzantines' answers to the problem they so frequently set themselves—that of relating man to the divine. They used the concept freely. We have seen how it was used to explain the majesty of the imperial office: the emperor was the iconic image of Christ. So was the patriarch. So was the ecstasy-seized monk. The sacred hierarchy of the court was an icon of the universe, while each Christian was physically the image of God, condemned to live in one world and hope for the other.

Generally we think of the icon in its religious context, and this is understandable. The icon as it was finally developed to be used in the Byzantine church was the most visible and dramatic presentation of the type. In the fully articulated iconic scheme, the walls of the church were mystically erased—covered and eliminated—by a whole program of icons, all arranged in a prescribed order. On the lower levels, immediately above the worshipers, appeared the Old Testament patriarchs and the saints; above them the great cycle of feasts; then the Apostles; at last the figures of most power, the Virgin and Christ himself. The Christian universe was thus effectively reproduced, and each icon, from the lowest to highest, cast on the viewer the special portion of divinity which lay behind it, so that the physical image dissolved and an awesome holy link was established. Adoration reached up; God's grace flowed down.

This was the theory, but we know just enough about the mentality of the mass of Byzantine Christians to guess at some difficulties. First, the average Byzantine was not versed in Neo-Platonism, nor was he a theologian, though the level of theological literacy in Byzantium was always exceptionally high. He knew that the images were holy, for no one doubted this, but was this only because of what they reflected? We gather from some of the *Lives* of the Byzantine saints, an important source for the life of the commons, that the ordinary Christian kept a much more physical focus in his personal religion. The amulet touched by a holy man, the remnants of a saint's body or clothing, and the icon of rich workmanship or materials, representing a holy figure or event—all were precious *in themselves,* and were accordingly not merely venerated but sincerely worshiped for the Divine Presence which was not beyond them but *in* them. The theory behind icons considered them identical with the prototype—whatever was figured—in *meaning.* The mass of believers saw icons and other physical manifestations of holiness to be the holy thing itself. This is the way the average Byzantine solved the riddle of the distance between human and superhuman. In his view the Christian could touch his God. This explains, for example, the fury of the popular opposition which met the Iconoclasts. With this warning, the idea of the icon can be examined in detail.

THE AIMS OF ART

There was a secular art in Byzantium. There are traces of it still surviving in the decorative floor mosaics found on the site of the Sacred Palace, for example, and in illustrated scientific manuals. Almost always, however, Byzantine art was religious art. There might be traces of older secular themes and techniques in this art, especially in manuscript illustrations; here for centuries a style recalling Hellenistic "illusionism" survived, with hints of natural space, natural light and shadow, and figures in three dimensions. The main currents of Byzantine art moved in other directions, however, and the aims of Byzantine art were, in the main, formed by religious preconceptions.

The Byzantine icon is a monument to these preconceptions. It was, first of all, independent of the craftsman who created it, independent of any personal or subjective creative desires he may have had. The icon was not his creation at all, but was a copy of a Type, a Type which reflected holiness as the shadow follows the substance. To copy an icon was an act of adoration, like prayer, and the painter of icons or worker in mosaic prepared to do his work in a sacramental atmosphere.

The history of icon-making is surrounded by legendry, especially of the icon "not made by hands." The first and most sacred of these was the Mandyllion of Edessa (called the Handkerchief of Veronica in the Western Church), the impress of Christ's face on a piece of cloth. Other icons were created in visions, by the saint who was to be portrayed, or so the artist who had the vision reported.

These Types naturally set the inescapable pattern for all icons which followed. Technical skill was desirable in an icon-maker, but not originality. Originality was unthinkable, for no man, whatever his artistic insights or sensibilities, would willingly tamper with divinely created forms.

The iconic figures which were set into the walls of Byzantine churches pose special problems, which will be dealt with in time. *All* icons, however, fixed or portable, follow a set of conventions, varying somewhat through the centuries, but coherent enough to mark the art which resulted as distinctly Byzantine. Of these conventions, three are primary: the handling of space, the use of light, and the feeling or use of time.

1. The Byzantine icon reveals a unique treatment of space, both of the space within the icon and the space which relates the viewer to the object viewed. Within the icon the human figure, or whatever figure is the subject, completely dominates background or environment. When the background is treated at all, it is reduced to a few allegorical or cryptic objects; it is obvious that the icon-masters were not concerned with reproducing "real" objects to surround the central image. In the so-called classical icon, figures may be casually related to one another, but we are aware of no treatment of perspective *within* the icon. Byzantine perspective, actually, is not ours; it is understandable only by recognizing that the icon is related visually to the *viewer*, not to some point behind the composition.

Byzantine "reversed" perspective derives from their theory of sight, where the act of seeing is a "shooting of shafts" from the eye. Because each figure is related to the eye of the viewer, space within the icon has no meaning. Figures overlap, walk on different planes, tread on each others' toes. They are turned, as well, so that the face and especially the eyes are always visible. Through the magical contact of the icon's eye with the viewer's eye an important effect of the image is transmitted.

The Byzantines were serious students of the Hellenistic science of optics. Their theories of sight lay behind a number of interesting technical devices, while fitting as well into a broader theory of aesthetics. The icon which was produced, however, represented an idea higher than all of these. Its figures—isolated, oriented to the viewer, obeying a "sacred" perspective which made Christ or the Virgin larger than their servitors—in all cases expressed not an artistic truth, but a theological one.

2. The Byzantines were faced with the problem of combining, in icons, both physical light and the divine light for which the icon served as a vehicle. Here, again, technique evolved to the point where the physical fact was made more reminiscent of a higher glory: in the use of mosaic, in the metallic highlights and the background or outline of gold, in the placing of iconic figures or groups in relation to light sources, such as windows or lamps. Since any "real" background had disappeared, there was no light source within the iconic framework, and shadows and highlights became stylized—even reversed. Light, always an attribute of deity, was to be used to outline and emphasize, to mystify and clarify at the same time.

Mosaic is an especially difficult and lively medium, precisely because of its light-reflecting qualities, for each mosaic die, slightly tilted in relation to its fellows, breaks the light individually and produces its own bit of brilliance. When the mosaic die is covered with gold foil, the spectator's eye moves (as the Byzantines meant it should); when the wall surface itself is curved, the effect is that much more intense. The icons, floating free of the wall, strike each viewer separately; their colors and tones change, and the intervening space is magically charged. Magical rather than physical space is what the Byzantines consistently aimed at creating, and the interpenetration of physical and metaphysical light was both a cause and a desirable side-effect of magical space.

3. The third, related component enclosed in the Byzantine icon was time—or rather, its disappearance, for mortal time was wiped out by the sacred event. Iconic theory showed that the figures or happenings imaged on the walls of the Byzantine church were not commemorated. They were eternally *there*, beyond the image. No physical space was caught up in the icon; no human time was reflected there. Before the icon, within the church, the Christian viewer lost his body and his history, and became a soul bathed in the proof of heaven.

4. Three more parts of the iconic ensemble are worth a brief glance, pattern, color, and music. The Byzantines, mindful of their Hellenistic heritage, had a strong feeling for number and rhythmic order. Sacred numbers, the One, the Three, the Four, the Twelve, were not to be lightly disregarded. There was power in them, as well as in their arrangements, and in the total and eternal pattern of the universe—the procession ordained by God. In some corners of Byzantine art other traditions are vaguely remembered, but in sacred art a stately balance is usually found. Motion is rhythmic and hieratic, although in later centuries a sort of Byzantine baroque style lent more nervous excitement to the figures and their arrangement. Repetition and balance were the norm, so that in this dimension, too, the icon repeated the thought of the guiding mind of the world.

The use of color by the Byzantines might have been included with their theories and uses of light, for color to them was light broken into its constituents. The Byzantine color-sense, however, was remarkably subtle and well developed; and their consciousness of symbolic color lent a particular flavor to their iconography. The colors of mosaics, marbles, or other objects such as silk and brocade tapestries, now mostly lost, are still preserved for us in descriptions which glory in hyperbolic Greek—and in the tints themselves. Color excited the imagination of the stodgiest monk, and authors with a more poetic turn of mind gloat over the nuances of glowing color in precious stones, over the effects of different tones of white—the white of milk, of snow, of old or new ivory, of silver—or of the varieties of gold and yellow, or the great range of reds and purples and blues. The Byzantine icon-maker might change his palette in the course of the centuries or according to different traditions; certain provincial mosaics, in Sicily and in the eleventh century examples surviving on the island of Chios, tend toward deeper, more dramatic and contrasting tones; the range of color used in the thirteenth and fourteenth centuries is more lapidary and sophisticated; but at all times the eye of the icon-maker was dominated by a color-hunger we can only guess at. His aim, of course, was not realism but richness and harmony, especially harmony.

The tones of color and the tones of music, both subject to the perfect laws of harmony, were felt by the Byzantines to be necessarily complementary. This civilization, with all its emphasis on sight and light, had to feel the attraction of the Word, and thus of sound and the sense of hearing. Both color and sound gained their beauty from the proper resolution of separate notes, and the aesthetic similarity of Byzantine sacred music to iconic art is becoming clearer now, as this music is being slowly recovered. Again, we do not hear their music as the Byzantines did, but in what we have heard, one discovers the unmistakable quality of mosaic, of harmonies resolving in the mind, of subtle colors, whose source is never exactly determined, and need not be.

THE CHURCH AS ICON

All the iconic elements went to fill and make significant a church structure which itself is of prime importance in Byzantium. As the Byzantine church-type developed, a number of theological and even philosophical dogmas were given concrete form, and it is obvious that the church existed, principally, to give them form.

To build or refurbish a church was naturally a pious act; in Byzantium, especially when the emperor was the donor, it was an architectural ritual as well, in which men repeated the pure forms of the universe. Nowhere is the Byzantine subordination of technique to theory better seen than in the most magnificent church ever constructed by this civilization: Justinian's Hagia Sophia. Built, like other imperial churches, to be a particular sign of the ordering of the secular world to match the work of God, Justinian's church was conceived not as a problem in monumental architecture or engineering, but as an exercise in solid geometry. The most perfect patterns were to be joined together to make an awe-inspiring symmetry. The designers directed, craftsmen labored, and the church has stood for 1400 years. The technical mistakes made in erecting it seem, by pure chance, to have canceled each other out.

Lesser Byzantine churches kept up the tradition in their own way. The Byzantine church, first of all, was built from the inside out. Its first principle was volume, not mass, or a number of related, spherical volumes surrounded by the containing shells of masonry or brick, and topped by a dome or domes that were often masked from the outside. Whatever the pedigree of the domed church, by the time it was fixed in a Byzantine mode its meaning was clear. It was the Type of the tomb of Christ; its hollow spaces descended from the martyr churches and the baptistries, with their parallel messages of death and future life. The church represented the greatest death and the greatest victory. It was also the Type of the universe. Its architectural elements swept up past the altar, where men worshiped, through the regions of the Apostles, through the realm of serving angels, to the dome and to God. The closed, curved forms of the Byzantine church thus prefigured the absolute merging or coalescence of all lives and of the end of every life.

Through its containing forms, the services and rituals which filled it in the never-ending cycle of Christian feasts, and the silent, continuous ritual of physical and spiritual contact between the viewer and the iconic program on the walls, the Byzantine church itself was turned into an image. Stone, marble, and mosaic, light penetrating and light reflected, color, sound, all defined and filled the cavelike spaces, and pointed the Byzantine believer on to the true shape and substance of paradise. The church, as an icon, was another artifact of this civilization, devoted to an idea we will return to, the cultivation of eternity.

Practicality and Impracticality

One of the most irritating, and stimulating aspects of Byzantine civilization is its refusal to respond to our labels or categories. "Practicality" by rights should be opposed to "impracticality," or the physical to the superhuman; there should be a perceptible tension. There are plenty of tensions in East Rome, but not often where we would expect to find them. The Byzantines were capable of creating fully articulated, sophisticated systems for solving the problems which faced their state. We see, as well, their ready willingness to abandon every material advantage, every physical device, and throw themselves into the hands of superhuman agencies. Yet no unbearable strain appeared to have afflicted them. The Byzantine operated effectively in the world; then, without a perceptible shift or break in attitudes, he left it. The machinery devised by the Byzantines to insure the survival of their Empire had a cold and awe-inspiring efficiency, and yet the Byzantines never deified efficiency. Here we might elaborate on two aspects of the Byzantine genius for a certain kind of organization, and then look at the other side—or is it the same?

THE TECHNIQUES OF SURVIVAL

BYZANTINE DIPLOMACY

The foreign relations of the Empire were conducted according to a pattern which should be familiar: strict attention to detail backed by a theory of metaphysical grandeur. For example, the logothete of the Drome, the key figure in the conduct of Byzantine diplomacy up through the eleventh century, carried this double burden; he had charge of all the practical details of getting information from all sources, interpreting, supplying and housing foreign dignitaries; at the same time he held a central ceremonial role, especially in the imperial audiences which showed, in ritual, the relationship of the Empire to those outside it.

Byzantine diplomacy rested on the firmest of pragmatic foundations—that it was better to talk than fight. War, though often fought and always threatening, was wasteful of Christian lives and of the substance of the Empire. Embassies, therefore, came and went, protected by their ancient sacrosanctity; and treaties defined the exact relations between East Rome and the nations. The Byzantine ambassador was rarely what we would call a professional diplomat. He might be drawn from any branch of the civil or military services, or from the clergy. He had no connection with the professional bureaus under the logothete. He was, in fact, an elevated messenger boy, for the amount of negotiating he could do was strictly circumscribed by his imperial master. Plenipotentiary ambassadors were unknown in the fully developed Byzantine system, where the emperor's personal responsibility for all acts of state was never lost to view.

The treaties which the diplomats of the Empire labored to arrange were meant to adjust every point of contact between the Empire and the other signatory power—frontier lines, commercial relations, military matters, and occasionally religious matters as well. Once drawn up, the treaties were ratified and sworn to by means of a complicated system of mutual oaths and the exchange of copies. The period during which the treaty was to have power varied from 5 years to 30, or even 50.

Behind these formal documents we see shadowy evidences of the administrative agencies which handled the everyday minutiae of diplomacy. The corps of interpreters was always important and must have been huge; its chief became a dignitary in his own right in the later years of the Empire. The variety of peoples the Byzantines dealt with called for linguists in every known tongue—interpreters of Germanic dialects and Persian in the sixth century, of Arabic, Slavic dialects, the Caucasian languages, and Latin later. From the sixth century on, East Roman contact with Turkic peoples made knowledge of that linguistic group necessary. Interpreters evidently were ranked. The least skillful acted as dragomans for foreign mercenaries or merchants; the most skillful drew up the imperial treaty documents, or translated during the receptions and ceremonies involving foreigners.

Other bits of machinery sometimes come to light, such as the Office for Barbarians, which must have had control of the care, feeding, and surveillance of foreign diplomats and their following. All barbarians were, as a matter of course, segregated from the population; diplomats more so, for it was assumed, correctly, that one of their jobs was espionage. In this respect, we have evidence that the Byzantines collected intelligence vigorously on both friend and foe. One of the prize sources for Byzantine diplomacy, Constantine VII's *On the Administration of the Empire*, gives us chapter and verse from the Byzantine diplomatic archives: tribal affiliations and alliances, geographical and economic data, political intelligence, and tactical suggestions on how to deal with difficulties. How all this information was collected we can only guess, although occasionally a genuine covert agent pops up in the writings of one of the Byzantine historians. There is a strong likelihood that foreign operations of this sort fell into the province of the logothete of the Drome.

What gave form and purpose to Byzantine diplomacy, however, to all the treaties, embassies, administrative actions and details, was the hierarchic, artificially stabilized Byzantine view of the secular world. All was directed according to this scheme and, as always, the technical competence of civil servants was reinforced by ritual and mystery. The pyramid of princes who owed vassalage or tribute to the Empire was set in place by the precise formulas of imperial documents called *chrysobulla* (the "golden seals"), by diplomatic ceremonial, by the marriage tie, by the granting of dignities, and especially by investment with the insignia of rule—the regalia. The subtleties worked into the collection of subordinate rulers (and thus subordinate nations) need not be discussed. We can see that the emperor's act of granting a crown and royal robes to a certain ruler gave East Rome a very concrete hold over that ruler. At the other end of the spectrum, there is a mere suggestion that the conversion of a pagan people to Christianity put that people under the emperor. Byzantine diplomacy, in brief, was a many-toned instrument, capable of playing the most intricate scores.

THE MILITARY

If the Byzantines preferred negotiations to fighting, they also preferred, if war came, to win. The professionalism of the Byzantine army at the height of the Empire's power was a phenomenon in the medieval world. If there were strategic limitations which the Byzantines ordinarily set themselves—ordinarily, that is, they fought defensive wars—the technical and theoretical framework they developed was admirable.

The Byzantine armed forces in their "classical" formation were divided into three sections: the screening force which held the frontiers, the thematic troops, settled in the themes and subject to instant recall, and the tagmatic, or household troops—8000 or more cavalry based in and around the capital. To these we can add the naval units (there were naval themes); Byzantium's navy, however, was a sometime thing. The Byzantine elite soldiery was the heavy cavalry (*cataphractoi*); each of the themes, in the tenth century, provided about 6000 of these heavy horsemen, plus infantry. The eastern or Anatolian themes furnished the cream of the army.

How this army was used depended naturally on the skill of the commanders and the nature of the opponent, but the Byzantines had no lack of expert technical advice and assistance. We know of manuals on the art of war, which carefully differentiated between the troops and tactics to be used against the Arabs, the Bulgars, the steppe nomads, and the Franks. The East Roman general could depend on a well-organized service of supply, expert engineers, and even an ambulance corps—imperial troops were valuable property, not to be left lying about on the battlefield. When its leadership was active and skillful the Byzantine army was able to mount brilliant operations. Involved amphibious actions, for example, retook Crete from the Arabs in the tenth century; Bulgaria was several times shattered by the confluence of combined arms when naval raids up the Danube aided the advance of cavalry columns from the south. In the ninth century the theory of the correct use of thematic regiments was fully justified when an invading Arab army was slowed, surrounded, and annihilated by the clockwork convergence of all the thematic corps—perhaps 100,000 men.

The weaknesses to which this first-class military machine succumbed have already been suggested. Theories of generalship remained, even after the heart of the vital thematic system dissolved; small masterpieces were fought with mercenaries and a few native troops after the doom of the Empire was all too clear and close. Enough of the Byzantine military tradition was visible during the First

Crusade, for example, to give rise to mutual contempt on the part of both Byzantines and Westerners: one tradition seemed cowardly, the other a comfort to brave idiots.

THE FLIGHT FROM REALITY

We ought to know enough about Byzantium by now to recognize that every advance on the side of practicality will usually be balanced—or overbalanced—by the Byzantine lack of concern for these very advantages.

The principal skew, or element of unreality, in the Byzantine military tradition is clear throughout the life of the Empire. Despite a realistic approach to tactics, men and equipment, supply, or medical care, the victory of any Byzantine army was in God's hands. The emperor, as God's image, might lead it; if not, he might designate anyone, casting his divinely inspired choice on, perhaps, a trusted bureaucrat. The proof of piety was in victory; there were some resounding defeats. The Byzantine view of Providence in battle worked against them on too many occasions, for any sign of the divine displeasure could rout their finest army. Here, as elsewhere, the belief in the absolute and incomprehensible power of God could thrust aside the most carefully contrived works of man.

Again, at all times, the Byzantine, from the emperor to the peasant, felt the temptation to leave the world. Or rather, in this desire the emperor was no more than any of his subjects: a sinner, "crucified to the world." Many Byzantines, first and last, turned without regret to the cultivation of their own souls, leaving behind power and responsibility. In the eleventh century the writer and politico Michael Psellos, who has left us invaluable personal notes on his times, tried a monastery. It didn't suit him, but it suited one of his friends, the lawyer Xiphilinus, perfectly. Xiphilinus, who was later made patriarch, despite his violent objections, was the more typical Byzantine.

The emperor whose reign was ended by the most treacherous plot, against which he made no resistance, the farmer who handed over a plot of land to a monastery and became a monk, were both obeying a singularly powerful impulse. It is this impulse which may have been behind the feebleness of the Byzantine defense against the Turks when the final days came. The world of sense could be engaging, pleasant, amusing; the world of the mind challenging and prestigious; the other world, where the soul's care was paramount, exercised a much more imperative pull, as long as Byzantium existed.

THE DENIAL OF TIME AND HISTORY

To say that the Byzantines denied, or seriously amended, "normal" conceptions of both time and history is *probably* not overstating the case. The variety of the components of Byzantine culture is nowhere more obvious than here. Patterns which show one attitude with respect to time and history are rejected elsewhere, and the result is a confusion which the Byzantines comfortably accepted, but which we find highly aggravating. The question raised, however, is a crucial one. Even beginning to understand a civilization as complex as the Byzantine means that we must know how they related their present to their past, and to what end they thought they were moving—*if*, in fact, they thought in these terms at all.

BYZANTINE HISTORIOGRAPHY

Since the Byzantines *wrote* history it would seem that they accepted the existence of history—a sequence of meaningful events meaningfully organized, a "past." Yet we know that they did not experience or "feel" history as we do; that they did not isolate unique causes and effects; that, especially, they were not conscious, as we are, of the "irreversibility of events."

Who wrote Byzantine history? Certainly there was a strong secular tradition, represented by such figures as the civil servant Procopius in the sixth century; Anna Comnena, who wrote in exquisite Greek of her imperial father's deeds in the twelfth century; the courtier Michael Psellos. Most Byzantine history surviving to us, however, takes the form of "world chronicles" written by monks—George, calling himself "the Sinner," for example, or Theophanes "the Confessor." In short, the Byzantine historical tradition was carried in large part by a group separated from secular currents and the secular mentality.

The world chronicle dealt only with the events of a given year. How were these years—the passage of time—measured and distinguished? Byzantine time notations are varied and particularly casual. There were several linear notations, i.e., time measured from the moment of Creation as the Byzantines calculated it. More often used was an "indiction" figure, but these indictions are not the most reliable chronological base points, for an indiction was a 15-year period originally used as a basis for recalculating tax revenues. Regnal years, figured from the time an emperor first assumed office, are more reliable. Still, what sort of consciousness of the absolute passage of time is revealed here? Time calculated from the Creation is presumably Christian time, which moves on to the Apocalypse, and then ceases. Time figured in regnal years, however, ends with the reign and begins again with the new emperor's accession. Indictions are not even tied to a successive chronology; they are 15-year cycles which go on forever, like taxation itself.

The attitudes toward history of the historians themselves might be taken into account. The monkish chroniclers invariably borrowed from whichever of their predecessors was available; what they wrote was not meant to be specifically theirs. They wrote, simply, so that "these events (all events, undistinguished except when the Divine Hand was seen in them) might not be lost to mankind." The approach was vaguely didactic: mankind needed somehow to know what had gone before. The secular, individualistic Procopius, on the other hand, who is careful to identify himself and his personal observations (in the tradition of Herodotus), seemed to feel (in the tradition of Thucydides) that the events which he recorded were very likely to be repeated.

Byzantine historiography, predictably, was an amalgam of the classical and Hellenistic tradition, with its cyclical form and individualistic emphasis, and a particular Christian view. The latter, insofar as it tolerated history at all, had a strong apocalyptic tone; it was disaster-prone, or prone to report disasters. The patterns to be found in existence were not human patterns. The works of men were not good, or even very important.

THE SENSE OF CONTINUITY

Again, in positioning themselves in history, or in being conscious of a past, the Byzantines avoid terms we would recognize. To them there had been no substantial, essential change in the organization of the world since Constantine the Great—no cultural overturn since, perhaps, Homer. Occasionally the turning years brought the necessity not of change but of *renovatio*—renewal. The importance of their Empire was not that it moved in any direction but that it existed forever. Under a Christian Caesar the citizens of this Empire continued to be Romans—the idea of the passage of Empire to a "Third Rome," put forward by the Muscovites in the fifteenth century, was, as has been noted, a profoundly un-Byzantine idea, for the Byzantines could not think of their city or their civilization as a "Second Rome."

The unwillingness of intelligent Byzantines to recognize that they were not Homeric or even Alexandrian Greeks is amusing, but we must also recognize that the Byzantines were not trying, like the Humanists of the Renaissance, to *revive* a Golden Age. Byzantine self-confidence is intimidating. Their world, as they saw it, was not *culturally* distinct from that of Alexander or Caesar, though it might be distinct *spiritually*. Most of man's important activities went on as they always had. Educated men partook of an unbroken heritage, Christian and pagan, and expressed themselves in the forms and language of that heritage. In such areas as scientific inquiry, Byzantium went so little beyond the corpus of theory which it had received from the Hellenistic scientists that we can say that there was no specifically Byzantine science at all—only a reception and continuation of what had been given. One part of the Byzantine mentality, then, conceived of time without successive periods, and thus without extension, in either past or future.

TIME, CEREMONY, AND RITUAL

If there is any clarity to be found in this frustrating subject, it appears that two views, or constructions, of time existed in Byzantium, and that neither much resembles our modern "historical" structure or pattern. Byzantine ritual and Byzantine ceremony, taking ritual as the sacred drama and ceremony as the secular drama, lead us to the following.

The "apocalyptic" or linear Christian time, such as that reflected in the world chronicles, was not the only sacred time available. (This linear time, with the Christian elements removed, is the basis for modern historical time: the background against which history is played out, forever.) We have already seen that the Byzantines felt uncomfortable with the historic, human events in the life of Christ (p. 60). The recollection of the events of that life—the sacred liturgical sequence—then was transformed, in Byzantium, into glimpses of eternity: a divine timelessness. The Supper, with Christ forever present, had always been and would always be. The icons depicting the other acts of Christ, and figuring the other sacred actors, expressed acts and persons which the Byzantines had taken *out* of history. They may have begun, but they never ended.

As a complement to these views of several sorts of sacred time, there is the secular ceremonial and the pre-Christian view contained in it. The great series of secular ceremonies had a thought behind them: that man, through them, renewed and continued time. Thus along with their view of the Empire as an absolute, eternal *fact*, the Byzantines seemed to feel that man, by his acts, can and must refresh and renew that Empire. The coronation ceremony was certainly the most vital of these acts, for, in it, a new sovereign created a new world. None, however, was superfluous. The imperial audiences, the ritual-laden appearances in the Hippodrome—all, by their explicit ordering and measuring of the world, arranged the proper flow of time. This relic of pagan thought existed without discomfort in Christian Byzantium. More, the cyclical, recurrent nature of time so affected the Byzantines that they were willing to amend Christianity itself to suit it. They were continually tempted by the sacred cosmogony of Origen, the great theologian and heretic of the third century, who saw not a single, linear progression from Creation to Judgment, but a cyclical series of Creations and Judgments, with a total salvation, proving the mercy of God, at the end of each age.

SELECTED BIBLIOGRAPHY

Anyone who wants to look more closely at the entire sweep of the history of the Byzantine Empire, or at individual historical problems and areas, can examine the following books. They should be available in a good public library. A number of them have been published in paperback format.

BARKER, ERNEST. *Social and Political Thought in Byzantium from Justinian I to the Last Palaeologus: Passages from Byzantine Writers and Documents.* Oxford University Press, 1957. The only collection we have of translated materials from the Byzantine authors themselves—selective, but extraordinarily valuable. "Social" thought is actually less well represented here than political.

BAYNES, NORMAN H. *Byzantine Studies and Other Essays.* Oxford University Press, 1960. Some original interpretations and tentative suggestions on how to look at Byzantium, by a wide-ranging scholar. This book might profitably be used with the one by Barker listed above.

BAYNES, NORMAN H. and H. ST. L. B. MOSS (eds.). *Byzantium: Introduction to East Roman Civilization.* Oxford University Press, 1948 (paperback). This is a collection of essays and, as such, is predictably spotty. The separate examination of such areas as law, administration, and religion can be helpful, however, and the impact of Byzantium on southern and eastern Europe is included.

BURY, J. B. *History of the Later Roman Empire from the Death of Theodosius I to the Death of Justinian.* 2 vols. Dover Publications, 1957 (paperback). Bury's old work is still useful; a solidly factual, classically written account of the Late Roman (or Early Byzantine) Empire to the death of Justinian.

DIEHL, CHARLES. *Byzantium: Greatness and Decline,* tr. by Naomi Walford. Rutgers University Press, 1957. There are other works of the great French Byzantinist translated and available, but this book is probably his most thoughtful attempt at explaining the strengths and weaknesses of the civilization. His thoughts are clearly put, if unimaginative. A valuable bibliography is arranged topically.

OSTROGORSKY, GEORGE. *History of the Byzantine State.* Rutgers University Press, 1957. The best work we have in English on the history of Byzantium as a political entity. This is a hefty, scholarly book, with thorough annotations and bibliography, but with only a passing concern for the central ideas of the civilization.

VASILIEV, ALEXANDER A. *History of the Byzantine Empire.* 2 vols. University of Wisconsin Press, 1960 (paperback). Vasiliev's work deals with the literary, artistic, and wider cultural impact of Byzantium, as well as "straight" history, but this is an older work, outdated in some respects. The bibliography has limited usefulness.

To these titles we might add:

GIBBON, EDWARD. *The Triumph of Christendom in the Roman Empire.* (*Decline and Fall of the Roman Empire,* chaps. 15–20) ed. by J. B. Bury. (Torchbooks) Harper & Row, 1958. The edition of this work prepared by J. B. Bury is the best to be found. Gibbon was, of course, absolutely antagonistic to the Byzantines, but his prose is always worth reading, and Bury's extensive notes have great value.

HUSSEY, JOAN. *The Cambridge Medieval History,* vol. IV. Cambridge University Press. The older edition of the great *Cambridge Medieval History,* 1927, is still valuable as a reference work. The new volume IV, edited by Joan Hussey, is now available.

Two problematical personalities, the emperors Constantine and Justinian, raise a series of questions on the decisive role of the emperor, the interplay of individual intent and historical forces. Specifically, how were Christianity and the imperial idea combined by Constantine and his successors? What were the effects of the move to the East? What vitiated Justinian's later attempt to renew the Roman world?

BURCKHARDT, JACOB. *The Age of Constantine the Great,* tr. by Moses Hadas. Doubleday Anchor Books, 1956. Burckhardt casts his net widely over the crisis of the late third and early fourth centuries before he deals with Constantine, who is described as an astute politician, not a Christian hero.

DOWNEY, GLANVILLE. *Constantinople in the Age of Justinian.* University of Oklahoma Press, 1960. Downey's small book is a first-class examination of the Imperial City under Justinian: the setting, the melding of traditions, social pressures, the new directions of Christianity.

JONES, ARNOLD H. M. *Constantine and the Conversion of Europe.* Collier-Macmillan Library Service (paperback), 1962. Jones is more narrowly concerned with the problem of "Constantine and Christianity," and gives a good resume of the latest scholarship on the subject.

PROCOPIUS. *The Secret History,* tr. by Richard Atwater. Ann Arbor Books, 1961. The "unpublishable" addition to Procopius' great history of the wars of Justinian. A gaudy and rather untrustworthy book, in the tradition of Suetonius.

URE, P. N. *The Age of Justinian.* Penguin Books (now out of print, but often available). Ure gives a good conventional synopsis of Justinian's reign; his book is really a commentary on the histories of Procopius (who can be read in his entirety in the Loeb Classical Library series).

The puzzle of the reasons for the passing of the classical order of things and the birth of the medieval construct still engages us—and an additional complication is involved in placing Byzantium within this context. Was Byzantium a part of "medieval" civilization at all? Did it act as an example and reservoir of ideas, or as the conscious opponent of a new and separate system, or both?

BARK, WILLIAM C. *Origins of the Medieval World.* Doubleday Anchor Books, 1960. Bark's essays emphasize the completeness of the break between the old Mediterranean Empire and the new order in the West; also the completeness of the separation between the medieval East and the medieval West.

CHAMBERS, M. (ed.). *The Fall of Rome: Can It Be Explained?* Peter Smith Publisher, 1961. A broad-gauge treatment of the various explanations offered by historians for the Fall.

DAWSON, CHRISTOPHER. *The Making of Europe.* Meridian, 1956. Byzantium here becomes the static society, rigid and brittle, as compared with the organically developing West, its structure provided by the church.

KATZ, SOLOMON. *The Decline of Rome and the Rise of Medieval Europe.* Cornell University Press, 1955. A more or less straightforward account of the collapse of the unitary Empire in the West and its fragmented legacy.

LOT, FERDINAND. *The End of the Ancient World and the Beginning of the Middle Ages.* (Torchbooks) Harper & Row, 1961. An account emphasizing the absolute division between the old Empire and its successors. The new forces, according to Lot, would be Islam, the papacy, and vassalage.

MOSS, HENRY ST. L. B. *The Birth of the Middle Ages.* Oxford

University Press (paperback), 1963. Moss stresses the inevitability of certain developments: the failure of Justinian, the evaporation of "personality," the return to primal, or primary, forces in the West. The comparison with Byzantium is implicit rather than overt.

For a fuller paperback bibliography of Islamic history and ideas, see the books in this series. Here we might ask what the general (unique or inherited) characteristics of Islam were; how its advent affected the Mediterranean balance of power; what conflicts and what junctures of ideas occurred between Islam and the Byzantine culture.

ANDREA, TOR. *Mohammed: The Man and His Faith,* tr. by Theophil Menzel. (Torchbooks) Harper & Row, 1960. Mohammed as a historical figure, with an assessment of the influences which reached him and of his influence on the religious history of the Near East.

BROCKLEMANN, CARL. *History of the Islamic Peoples.* Capricorn Books, 1960. The best brief history of Islam available, with an emphasis on the period before the rise of Ottoman power.

GIBB, HAMILTON A. R. *Mohammedanism: An Historical Survey* (2nd ed.). Galaxy Books, 1953. The elements of Islamic civilization–Koranic, traditional, legal–given their best brief treatment.

HAVIGHURST, ALFRED (ed.). *The Pirenne Thesis: Analysis, Criticism, Revision.* D. C. Heath and Company, 1958. A collection of reactions to the original thesis, centering mostly, as the thesis did, on the evidence of economic decline or continuity.

JEFFERY, ARTHUR (ed.). *Islam: Muhammad and His Religion.* (Liberal Arts Press) Bobbs-Merrill Company, 1958.

LEWIS, BERNARD. *The Arabs in History.* (Torchbooks) Harper & Row, 1960. Some remarks on the Arabs before Islam, an account of their advance to power, an analysis of the fragmenting of "Arabic" Islam along with an estimation of the cultural tradition which they left, all usefully set out.

PIRENNE, HENRI. *Mohammed and Charlemagne*. Meridian, 1957. Here Pirenne sets out his controversial claim that the unity of the Roman world was broken, not by the so-called decline of Rome but by the advance of Islam in the early seventh century, thus Mohammed inevitably led to Charlemagne.

ULLAH, N. (ed.). *Islamic Literature*. Washington Square Press, 1963. All these collections of the texts of Islam are useful; Ullah provides a more thorough commentary and analysis.

WILLIAMS, JOHN A. (ed.). *Islam*. Washington Square Press, 1963.

Byzantine civilization, the focus of this book, can be variously approached. How have historians usually searched for Byzantium's major cultural and political forces and symbols? What was the tone or principal harmonic of the Empire? What were the integrative and disintegrative forces within it which mark out its history?

GUERDAN, RENE. *Byzantium*. Capricorn Books, 1962. More imaginative, less solidly scholarly than Hussey or Runciman. Guerdan is at least open to the dramatic aspect of Byzantium and its intensely integrated view of the world.

HUSSEY, JOAN MERVYN. *The Byzantine World*. (Torchbooks) Harper & Row, 1961. A small book, about half of which is devoted to a capsule history of the Empire, but a good introduction to the principal themes of Byzantine life.

RUNCIMAN, STEVEN. *Byzantine Civilization*. Meridian, 1956. A straightforward and conventional treatment of the main divisions of the civilization. Chapters on Byzantine administration are more solid than those on cultural and social areas.

Byzantine Orthodox Christianity was one of the great creations and supports of the Empire, it was a force in opposition, and it was a legacy. We can ask: What seems to distinguish this church and its dogma within the framework of Christianity? How did its theologians come to form their views of salvation, Christian life, the church and (or in) the world? How was "imperial Christianity" possible, and why did this Christian system survive when the Empire itself perished?

BENZ, ERNST. *The Eastern Orthodox Church.* Doubleday Anchor Books, 1963. A committed book by a convert to Orthodoxy, biased, but sensitive to the original and unique characteristics of this type of Christianity.

FEDOTOV, G. P. *The Russian Religious Mind: Kievan Christianity, the Tenth to the Thirteenth Centuries.* (Torchbooks) Harper & Row, 1960. The first chapters of this work are recommended for the author's specific contrasting of Byzantine religiosity with that of medieval Russia, Byzantium's greatest missionary achievement.

LEBRETON, JULES, and JACQUES ZEILLER. *History of the Early Church,* vol. IV. Collier-Macmillan Library Service, 1962. A usable reference work for the centuries of Christianity which formed the "Byzantine" Christian view—currents, councils, dogmas.

SHEREGHY, BASIL. *The Divine Liturgy of St. John Chrysostom.* Liturgical Press, 1960. The liturgical sequence connected with the name of John "the Golden-Tongued" is the most commonly used, and the most Byzantine, liturgy of Orthodoxy.

WARE, TIMOTHY. *The Orthodox Church* (Pelican) Penguin Books, 1963. Ware is matter-of-fact in his approach to Orthodoxy, but has good insights into the philosophical background to its theology.

The study of Byzantine art raises special questions: What artistic points of view remained from the classical and Hellenistic eras, and why did they survive? What unique artistic or aesthetic vision was created? What could or could not be successfully exported, to the Slavic world or to the West? What in this art has now caught the imagination of the modern world?

G. LAZAREFF. *Russian Icons.* Mentor Books, 1962. Russian Orthodoxy soon developed its own artistic modes, but these icons have interest as an offshoot of Byzantine types and of the Byzantine "iconic" idea.

NEUMAYER, HEINRICH. *Byzantine Mosaics.* Crown Publishers, 1964. This small book almost overcomes the natural difficulties of putting color plates into a limited compass; the plates here are representative, and the brief introduction is perceptive.

RICE, DAVID TALBOT. *Art of the Byzantine Era.* Frederick A. Praeger, Publisher, 1963.

RICE, DAVID TALBOT. *Byzantine Art.* (Pelican) Penguin Books, 1961.

Two general introductory studies: the first is more concerned with the patterns and theories of Byzantine art and its offshoots; the second, an older work, handles the various categories. Both have black-and-white reproductions.

RICE, DAVID TALBOT. *Byzantine Frescoes from Yugoslav Churches.* (Mentor Books) New American Library of World Literature, 1963. Reproductions of thirteenth and fourteenth century fresco paintings from an important margin of the Empire, with a history of Byzantine art in this area.

It is suggested that anyone interested in the artistic phase of Byzantine civilization refer to the following, full-scale studies.

GRABAR, ANDRE. *Byzantine Painting.* (Skira) World Publishing Company, 1953. Mosaic and fresco, beautifully reproduced and with a continuing text by the foremost European student of Byzantine art.

RICE, DAVID TALBOT. *The Art of Byzantium.* Harry N. Abrams, 1959. A fairly brief descriptive survey, followed by good reproductions in color and a large number of monochrome plates, covering most aspects of Byzantine art, including the minor arts.

VOLBACH, W. F. *Early Christian Art.* Harry N. Abrams, 1962. As its title indicates, this book does not move much past the sixth century. It has a good selection of monochrome plates, a short introduction, and is more self-consciously a "picture book" than either Grabar or Rice's books.

INDEX